Cambridge Elements ☰

Elements in Religion and Violence
edited by
James R. Lewis
University of Tromsø
Margo Kitts
Hawai'i Pacific University

HUMAN SACRIFICE

Archaeological Perspectives from Around the World

Laerke Recht
University of Cambridge

CAMBRIDGE
UNIVERSITY PRESS

CAMBRIDGE
UNIVERSITY PRESS

University Printing House, Cambridge CB2 8BS, United Kingdom

One Liberty Plaza, 20th Floor, New York, NY 10006, USA

477 Williamstown Road, Port Melbourne, VIC 3207, Australia

314–321, 3rd Floor, Plot 3, Splendor Forum, Jasola District Centre,
New Delhi – 110025, India

79 Anson Road, #06–04/06, Singapore 079906

Cambridge University Press is part of the University of Cambridge.

It furthers the University's mission by disseminating knowledge in the pursuit of
education, learning, and research at the highest international levels of excellence.

www.cambridge.org
Information on this title: www.cambridge.org/9781108728201
DOI: 10.1017/9781108610322

First published 2019

A catalogue record for this publication is available from the British Library.

ISBN 978-1-108-72820-1 Paperback
ISSN: 2397-9496 (online)
ISSN: 2514-3786 (print)

Cambridge Elements

Human Sacrifice

Archaeological Perspectives from Around the World

DOI: 10.1017/9781108610322
Published online: December 2018

Laerke Recht

University of Cambridge

ABSTRACT: Sacrifice is not simply an expression of religious beliefs. Its highly symbolic nature lends itself to various kinds of manipulation by those carrying it out, who may use the ritual in maintaining and negotiating power and identity in carefully staged 'performances'. This Element will examine some of the many different types of sacrifice and ritual killing of human beings through history, from Bronze Age China and the Near East through Mesoamerica to Northern Europe. The focus is on the archaeology of human sacrifice, but where available, textual and iconographic sources provide valuable complements to the interpretation of the material.

KEYWORDS: sacrifice, Ancient Near East, China, Egypt, Mesoamerica

ISBNs: 9781108728201 (PB) 9781108610322 (OC)
ISSNs: 2397-9496 (online) 2514-3786 (print)

Contents

1 Introduction

Human sacrifice continues to fascinate. The apparently purposeless violence and death inspire awe and horror alike. Sacrifice has at least as many variations as cultures that have practiced it, and there are few universal elements to the practice. But one universal that can be stated with a fair degree of certainty is that sacrifice was in fact never perceived as purposeless by those performing it. The people involved kill – or die – for something they believe in. This is not so very far from modern ideals of dying for one's country. Ancient sacrifices may have been performed with all the fanfare of an Olympic Games opening ceremony, in many cases a carefully calculated and staged event, perhaps to induce horror, to impress, to negotiate or to maintain identities, power, and authority. However, such shows would not be effective without the underlying beliefs of the ritual act. Whatever one might think of the act itself, it has its own logic, much of which could only be read by cultures now lost to us. Left to us are traces in the ground, in images and on pages that we may try to piece together to simulate what once was.

Much of the material presented here will appear gruesome (and therein lies our fascination). However, a judicious comment on Mayan glyphs and art is applicable to everything discussed here: "As we decipher the writing system and decode the imagery, we are learning to understand this message, which, since it is not addressed to us or our sensibilities, is sometimes disturbing" (Schele and Miller 1992: 41). The purpose of this work is not to judge whether or not the acts represented by the material are gruesome, cruel, or immoral. Rather, it is to investigate this particular religious practice in some of its characteristic variations through time and space, as represented in the archaeological record. To attempt, as far as possible, to determine the actors involved, the manner of sacrifice, and most importantly, the kinds of contexts where it occurred.

It will be noted that the discussion throughout is marked by a cautious rhetoric, with words like 'possible', 'may', 'likely', 'appear/seem', and so on. This is of course due to the inherent uncertainties of the archaeological material, but equally to the controversial nature of the subject.

Typically, more stringent criteria are applied for sacrifice to be accepted as an explanation over others. One commentator has gone so far as to drag the material to a modern court, where it would not call for conviction (Briggs 1995). Much as this is a fair point, very few archaeological explanations would be able to pass through such a strict needle eye. The analogy of a modern court is a useful illustration for how the evidence for sacrifice is required to be stronger than alternative explanations. In other words: for a 'conviction' of sacrifice, the data has to be strong enough to prove this unequivocally, while other explanations do not usually need the same strength because they do not even require a trial. A revealing misunderstanding in this analogy is the idea of sacrifice as a crime, which also serves to show the inappropriateness of placing ancient contexts in such a modern setting. Conversely, it also happens that an eagerness to detect sacrifice leads to hasty conclusions as to its certain presence in some instances.

Be that as it may, nearly every example presented in these pages has met with alternative interpretations or outright denials. This is not simply due to the difficulty of unequivocal identification. Archaeology does not exist in a vacuum. It is part of the histories and identities of many peoples, and has been used for political, national, colonial, and racist agendas (most famously as part of Nazi propaganda, but also in more subtle ways even today – see, e.g., Fagan 2006; Pollock and Bernbeck 2005). As some of the material also relates more directly to living populations, especially in Mesoamerica, the issue can become a very sensitive and personal one (Mendoza 2007a).

Sacrifice has been the focus of many a grand theory, and the literature on these is far too extensive to do it justice here. Some of the most influential writers include Edward Burnett Tylor (sacrifice as gift, 1971), William Robertson Smith (sacrifice as communion, 2002), Henri Hubert and Marcel Mauss (sacrifice as mediation, 1964), René Girard (sacrifice as controlled violence, 2005), and Nancy Jay (sacrifice as male substitution for blood relations, 1992).[1] Elements of all of the theories proposed by these authors and others can explain part of the material that follows, but no single theory is so far a good explanation for all cases. This is more than anything a testament to the diversity of cultural contexts and types of sacrifice, and the importance of attempting to understand each example within its own context first of all.

In order to provide some guidance as to what is meant by the concept, I follow the same usage as previously, with sacrifice referring to a religious ritual where a living being is deliberately killed in the process for the purposes of the event and usually in honour of a supernatural entity (Recht 2014: 403 n. 3). Defined as such, it should be noted that sacrifice in a sense is an artificial category. That is, it is a modern construct. While I here consider both the deposits at the Teotihuacan Moon Pyramid and the Xibeigang cemetery at Anyang cases of human sacrifice, the people of Teotihuacan may not have thought that their actions were the same or even similar to those of Shang period Anyang, and vice versa. The term 'supernatural' is used because the entities to which sacrifices are made, or in whose name/honour they are made, do not always fit neatly into concepts such as gods and deities. Other out-of-this-world beings include ancestors, spirits, and possibly demons: the main point is that they are perceived as *agents*, still in some way able to influence the world of the living or requiring attention from this world to act in another one.

---

[1] For an excellent reader with excerpts from the most important theories of sacrifice, with introductory comments for each, see Carter 2003.

The term *killed in the process* is also important. While the death of the 'victim'[2] is part of the ritual, it is not necessarily the highlight or the reason for the act – on the contrary, the killing is a means to an end, whatever that end (gift, mediation, etc.). Thus, a communion (generally more applicable to animal sacrifice), or the manipulation/display of bones following the killing, may in fact be more important than the moment of death.

Identifying Sacrifice in Archaeological Contexts

Another step altogether is moving from theoretical definitions of sacrifice to identifying it archaeologically. To do this, it is necessary to identify the two main features: signs of a violent cause of death and signs of a sacred/religious context. These are very general criteria which must be placed in the broader context. In some cases, signs of both may not be sufficient, while in others, one or the other may be enough when combined with other, less direct data.

Cause of death is most explicitly determined by evidence of trauma, which can include stab wounds, cutmarks, fractured bones and, in the case of soft tissue, groove marks from a rope or stake. For the trauma to be related to the cause of death, it must be associated with the time of death. That is, it must be *perimortem*. Perimortem injuries can be difficult to differentiate from postmortem injuries, because in both cases, limited or no healing takes place (as opposed to antemortem injuries). One possible way of differentiating them is through the type of cut on a bone – whether it is consistent with known patterns of decapitation, scalping and butchering, or rather with later interference, such as from looters. However, in

---

[2] I do not like this term because it implies an asymmetrical relationship where the human/animal dying is always inferior and helpless, and the sacrificer superior and powerful. This is too simple a view for much of the material. However, I have not been able to find a better and equally effective referent.

many cases, the cause of death would leave no marks on the bones (in fact, such marks may represent the actions of a non-expert), so this direct evidence is not available to us.

Beside this, several suggestions have been made for more specific archaeological signatures of sacrifice for certain areas (Schwartz 2012: 13; Tiesler 2007), which bear repeating in a more general format because they are in fact what arguments for human sacrifice are very often based on. Thus, possible indications of human sacrifice in archaeological contexts include

- human skeletal remains in sacred contexts
- patterns in the skeletal remains suggesting a selective process, based on, e.g., age, sex, or bodily deformities
- simultaneous burial of several people, especially with either overall equal status or with one individual apparently treated differently; also signs of 'staging' the interments
- evidence of violence (cause of death, binding, other types of submission)
- human skeletal material associated with the construction of structures (especially foundations or later additions)
- similarity in treatment of animal and human skeletal remains, especially where sacrifice is suspected for the animal remains
- abnormal context/treatment of body in relation to the area and period[3]

None of these signatures is very strong on its own, and can in several cases be confused with other activities that leave similar signatures (e.g., 'secular' violence or actions related to ancestor worship). The combination of those related to violence and religion makes a stronger case, but still

---

[3] Some types of sacrifice will almost never be detectable archaeologically, and it is therefore not possible to say anything about their existence or nature. Sacrifices thrown into the sea or placed in the open would leave no traces, for example.

needs to be assessed individually and combined with analogous or contextual material from the area and/or period in question. For example, we can identify the northern European bog bodies of the last centuries BCE as abnormal burials because inhumation was not the common burial practice at this time and place. Without this context, the argument for sacrifice weakens significantly.

A Note on Types of Sacrifice and Terminology

While the examples of human sacrifice in what follows are incredibly diverse, some 'types' occur again and again. The geographically broadest type is that of mortuary sacrifice. Mortuary sacrifice is here understood as any human sacrifice related to funerals and later ritual activities in the same space, including those related to ancestor worship. If they do not take place within a clearly delimited mortuary space (usually a necropolis or cemetery, but not necessarily so), they may be harder to identify as such. An important sub-category of mortuary sacrifice is so-called retainer sacrifice, a phrase often repeated here. Retainer sacrifices are all mortuary sacrifice, with the further characteristic of being subordinate to some kind of 'master'. That is, they are individuals related to a main deceased (possibly as servants, slaves, family members, or substitutes for these) and sacrificed as part of this relationship.

Another fairly common type of sacrifice is associated with construction activities (much more common for offerings than human sacrifices). Typically, these have appeared in Near Eastern contexts in the foundations of buildings and are therefore often known as 'foundation deposits' (Ellis 1968). However, they are not always found exactly in the foundations of buildings, and therefore the phrases 'construction deposit' / 'building deposit' and 'construction sacrifice' may also be used.

Human Sacrifice and Archaeology

The current work is focussed on archaeological contexts. However, archaeology does not and should not exist in a vacuum, so where other sources have clear relevance and relation to the archaeological material, they are also discussed. This is particularly clear in terms of Mesoamerica, where iconography and glyphs add significantly to our understanding of the archaeological contexts. What is more, this is by no means a comprehensive survey of human sacrifice in archaeology. The five areas and periods have been selected to offer the most representative, compelling, and diverse examples of human sacrifice. Thus, the Near East is where we begin, and from there to China, via Egypt. Northern Europe's bog bodies will offer a complete change of scenery, as will the final stop in Mesoamerica. No claim is made concerning origins or influence from one place to another. On the contrary, human sacrifice had a local meaning for each of the groups in these places. Even if the idea first came from somebody having viewed the ritual in one place and bringing this back home (purely hypothetical; there is no evidence of this happening), the practice was adapted and fitted to local needs and ideology. For those familiar with the topic, notable omissions not included due to space are the data related to the Incas in South America, the Native American at Cahokia, and the burials at Kerma in Nubia, not to mention the tophets in Carthage and elsewhere. The appendix provides a selected bibliography as a starting point for learning more about these and others.

2 The Near East

We start in the Near East, with a place that has almost turned legend: Ur. The name itself evokes a sense of deep history, and still maintains its hold in the German *Urgeschichte* and the English *ur-* as referring to something

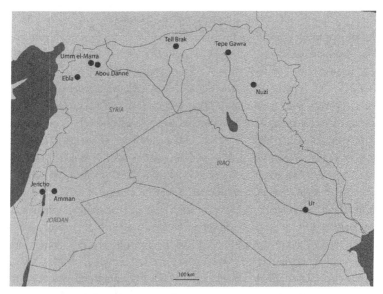

Figure 1 Map of the Near East with main sites mentioned in the text.

original.[4] The Royal Tombs at Ur present some of the earliest secure evidence of human sacrifice, and are almost invariably used as comparison in discussions on human sacrifice anywhere in the world. The largely untouched tombs present a wealth and beauty that have captured the imagination of public and scholars alike since their discovery by Sir Leonard Woolley in the 1920s. By any parameter, they are extraordinary, and although they are perhaps some of the best early evidence of sacrifice, earlier examples have been suggested, in very different contexts.

[4] See also Recht 2014: 413–426, from which much of the discussion in this section is adapted.

Foundation and Building Sacrifices

The deposition of offerings in conjunction with the construction of buildings is a well-known practice in the ancient Near East (Ellis 1968). Such deposits consist of object and sometimes animal remains. From early periods at the sites of Nuzi and Tepe Gawra, children were placed under floors and in association with walls, suggesting that they could also qualify as building deposits (al-'Ubaid to Old Babylonian period – see Green 1975: 59–79). For example, infants were found in walls, below floors, and in a doorway at Nuzi; in a later phase, 11 infants had been placed under the wall in the corner of a room, with a vessel inverted over the remains (Starr 1939: 9–10, 14, 16, 226–227, 267–268, 274–275, 298–299, 510). At Tepe Gawra, the infants were associated with temples: below floors, in walls, and directly in front (Tobler 1950: 57, 66, 100–101; Speiser 1935: 25–26, 140, 142, pl. XII).[5] These depositions are often explained as natural deaths, with a reference to high infant mortality rates. However, the Nuzi infants were all aged 3–12 months and sometimes occur in multiples, which indicates a selective process rather than the randomness of natural death (also more likely to be one at a time). In these cases, the location in liminal places is particularly interesting as such spaces are hotspots for ritual activity, especially sacrifice. If any of these infants were in fact sacrificed, they may themselves have been perceived as liminal individuals due to their youth.

Quite a different kind of foundation deposit may be represented at a later stage at Tell Abou Danné (c. 1800–1600 BCE – Tefnin 1979: 48–49). Here, a circular pit was part of the foundations of the fortifications. A human skeleton had been placed in it, with its back against the wall, along with several dog skeletons, including a very young puppy. This appears to be a fairly

[5] For other possible examples: Kudish Sagir, near Nuzi (Starr 1939: 9–10), Tell Brak (Mallowan 1947: 70; Matthews 2003: 196–197), Chagar Bazar (Mallowan 1936: 18), and Tell el-Kerkh (Tsuneki et al. 1998).

straightforward sacrifice related to the construction of the walls, and given their function as fortifications, the sacrifice may have had a protective purpose as well.

Retainer and Mortuary Sacrifices

When excavating the Early Dynastic cemetery at Ur, Leonard Woolley grouped 16 of the tombs as 'royal' due to shared characteristics that included their larger size, more elaborate construction and wealth of grave goods (often both in quantity and quality) (Figure 2).[6] One of the shared characteristics is also that they contained what he believed to be human sacrificial victims, killed at the funeral of their master and thus an example of 'retainer' sacrifice. More explicitly, human victims are mentioned for tombs PG 789, PG 800, PG 777, PG 779, PG 1157, PG 1648, PG 1618, PG 1332, PG 1050, PG 1054 and PG 1237. All architectural elements are not preserved in all the tombs, but based on the most complete ones, each is thought to consist of a main chamber, holding the body of the deceased or owner of the tomb, and a dromos or shaft with further offerings. Typically, the human victims were placed in this area, to the extent that it is also known as the 'death pit' of each tomb.

PG 789 may have belonged to King Meskalamdug (Woolley 1934: 62–71). The main chamber with the body of the deceased had been looted, but the 'death pit' contained a wealth of goods, animals, and humans (Figure 3). In the dromos were six 'soldiers', with copper spears and wearing copper helmets.[7] Behind them were six oxen, associated with two four-wheeled

---

[6] For suggested internal chronology and owners of each tomb, see Reade (2001) and Marchesi (2004). Woolley's meticulous publication (1934) still provides the best source and description of the tombs. See also Woolley 1954; 1982.

[7] The skulls and helmets had all been crushed flat: one of these is on display in the British Museum (BM 121414).

Elements in Religion and Violence

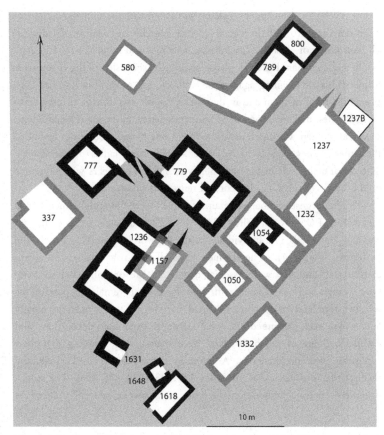

Figure 2 Ur Royal Cemetery (redrawn after Woolley 1982: 53).

wooden vehicles. One human skeleton was found with the animals (designated a 'groom') and two with the wagons (designated 'drivers'). A row of 'ladies', in all their finery of elaborate headdresses, earrings, and necklaces of gold, lapis lazuli, and carnelian, had been placed against the short side of the chamber, in a line with heads leaning against the wall. On top of them, a lyre had been placed. In front of them and in the rest of the pit was a mass of human and animal bones, making a total of 63 human skeletons in the pit. The additional men and women were each associated with fine items, though not as fine as the others. They appear to be more soldiers and 'ladies of the court'.[8] The remarkable finds include another lyre, bundles of spears with silver and gold heads, rein rings, bead-decorated reins, and wooden chests.

The largest number of retainers comes from the aptly named 'Great Death Pit', PG 1237 (Woolley 1934: 113–124). The main tomb of this pit was not identified. The individuals in the pit were all adults, six male and 68 female (Figure 4).[9] The six men were all in a row against the north-eastern wall and five were associated with an axe or knife. Below them, four women were associated with four lyres. The remaining part of the southwestern end of the pit contained the rest of the women in mostly neat rows, each in fine dress, with silver or gold hair decorations and jewellery. Some of the body parts were overlapping, proving that their deposition was simultaneous. A more modest example is PG 1648, the smallest of the royal tombs (Woolley 1934: 133–134, 405–406). The stone-structured main chamber contained its male owner centrally placed in

[8] Woolley supplies elaborate lists recording the exact finds with each body, as far as could be determined. In this case, see Woolley 1934: 65–67.

[9] Gender is in most cases determined by associated finds in the Ur material, rather than by osteological methods. As Vidale warns, gender does not necessarily match biological sex (2011: 432).

Elements in Religion and Violence

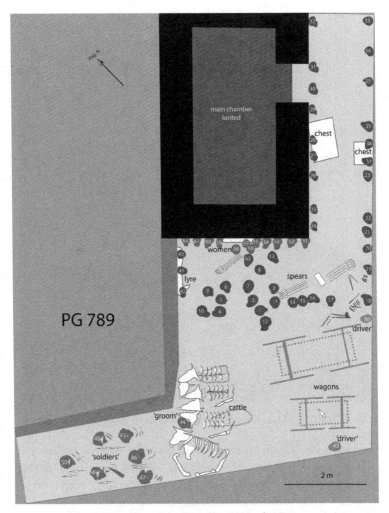

Figure 3 Ur PG 789 (redrawn after Woolley 1934: pl. 29).

Human Sacrifice

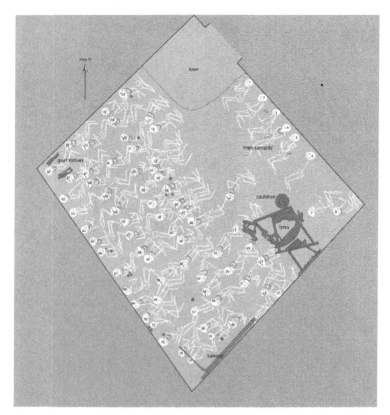

Figure 4 Ur PG 1237 Great Death Pit (redrawn after Woolley 1934: pl. 71).

a wooden coffin (Figure 5). Surrounding the coffin were the skeletons of two women and two men (with additional isolated bones from another adult and a child – Molleson and Hodgson 2003: 100), interpreted as 'attendants'. In a small forecourt, there were many sheep/goat bones.

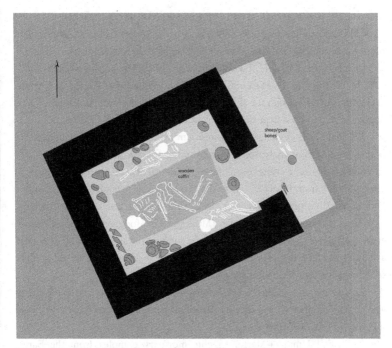

Figure 5 Ur PG 1648 (redrawn after Woolley 1934: Figure 26).

Woolley hypothesised that the retainers found in the Ur tombs had died by voluntarily drinking poison (1934: 35). He based this on the lack of any immediately visible trauma to the skeletons, their apparently peaceful postures, and the presence in several of the tombs of small bowls or cups. In many cases, one cup was associated with each skeleton, and a large cauldron was placed in PG 1237, which could have held the poison. Given the evidence at the time, this hypothesis is not unreasonable, but several factors speak against it. Most importantly, new research on two of the preserved skulls (female body 52 from PG 1237 and 'soldier' from PG 789) has shown that they had been subjected to blunt force trauma – that is, blows to the head by a sharp weapon like a pointed axe (Baadsgaard et al. 2011; Baadsgaard et al. 2012). The published plan of PG 1237 hints at further clues to violence and the manner of death: several of the skeletons are shown with the skull twisted around to the back, unlikely to have happened due to post-depositional displacement (Vidale 2011: 438).

Finally, the evidence for postmortem manipulation and arrangement of bodies continues to increase, thus accounting for the neat rows and overall careful display of the entire assemblages. Evidence of such postmortem manipulation comes from PG 1237, where the two lyres had been placed on top of the bodies. Possible preservative measures using heating and mercury sulphide have been detected in recent studies (Molleson and Hodgson 2003; Baadsgaard et al. 2011; Baadsgaard et al. 2012), and the study of the skull of the soldier with a helmet did not detect an impact hole in the helmet itself, meaning that somebody had put it on after his death (Vidale 2011: 439).

No other site in the Near East comes close to Ur in terms of the sheer wealth and number of sacrifices.[10] However, mortuary sacrifices have been suggested at several other sites.

At Tell Umm el-Marra, an elite mortuary complex from the Early Bronze Age (c. 2550–2200 BCE) consisted of tombs, so-called installations, and other related features (Schwartz et al. 2006; Schwartz 2012; 2013). The installations are structural features separate from the tombs, clearly part of the mortuary cult, but not necessarily built in conjunction with a human

---

[10] Burials at nearby Kish, slightly predating the Ur tombs, appear to have held similar contents, but were unfortunately too disturbed to draw conclusions and not as carefully excavated as the Ur tombs (see Gibson 1972: 83–86; Moorey 1978: 104–110).

burial. They are especially characterised by the presence of complete equids and puppies in varying numbers (equids up to eight, dogs up to six), but some also contained human infants, which could be interpreted as sacrifices. Installations A, B, C, and D all contained the remains of one to three infants, and two partial infant skeletons were also found outside Installation B.[11] The infants were in some cases associated with a spouted jar possibly used for libations, and in Installation D, partial remains of three infants were found inside a jar (Schwartz 2012: 19). The infants appear to have been deposited after the equids, and especially associated with the equid heads (Weber 2008: 502–504), leaving the impression that they were part of a cult that included the animals, possibly in some way subordinate to the equids, if not exactly sacrificed to them.

One of the tombs, Tomb 1, may also have contained sacrificial victims (Porter 2012: 201–202). The tomb consists of three layers (Schwartz et al. 2003: 330–341). The bottom held one adult, with bones disturbed by later burials. The middle layer held two adult men, one infant, and grave goods of silver objects, pottery, a dagger, and sheep/goat bones (Figure 6a). In the final and top layer were two adult women, two babies, and grave goods of gold objects, beads, lapis lazuli, a seal, cosmetic shells, pottery, and sheep/goat bones (Figure 6b). The top two layers consist of single deposits of multiple burials, which in their own right have to be explained. Considering the presence of infants, and comparison with the situation in the installations, sacrifice is a possible interpretation. It could also be the case that one of the layers is a sacrificial deposit in honour of the other one (the women, with the finer grave goods, could be seen as the 'main' burial; on the other hand, sacrifices are more commonly placed on top of or in some way 'after' the main burial). Porter also suggests that both top layers constitute sacrificial deposits (Porter 2012: 205).

[11] One was stillborn, so cannot have been killed as part of sacrificial ritual.

This would explain the apparent symmetrical and asymmetrical relations, based on gender, infants, grave goods, and position of bodies. The tomb does seem like a carefully thought-out unity, rather than a sequence of depositions placed as needed, and therefore this explanation is appealing. It could also provoke a reconsideration of the entire mortuary complex.[12]

Tombs at the ancient site of Jericho were excavated in the 1950s by Kathleen Kenyon (Kenyon 1960; 1964). Among the Middle Bronze Age tombs were several with multiple burials in a single tomb that seemed to have been placed simultaneously: Tombs G1, H6, H18, H22, P17, and P19 (Kenyon 1960: 443–469, 480–513; Kenyon 1964: 358–368, 388–410; Ellis and Wesley 1964: 695–696).[13] In G1, at least seven of the 22 individuals found had been buried at the same time. In H6, four individuals had been buried at the same time, with three of them seemingly centred on the fourth, thought to be a man buried with his wife and two children. Tomb H18 included 13 individuals buried simultaneously, one adult as the focus roughly in the centre, and another adult and 11 children to the sides, while H22 contained 12 individuals (four adults, six children) in a fairly neat row. Another neat row, this time of 18 skeletons, was found in P17 (Figure 7). Finally, Tomb P19 presents the unusual scenario of six individuals buried at the same time (male and female, aged 11–26) with blunt force trauma to the head, and three of them missing one hand.

Interlocking of limbs serves to support the single event argument in these cases. We see here a much more diverse demographic than at Ur, with

---

[12] Porter also presents another example from Shioukh Tahtani in Syria, where the burial of five individuals may all be interpreted as sacrificial (rather than the more standard retainer-type burial where four would be subsidiary to the fifth individual) (Porter 2012: 199–201).

[13] These tombs were in fact also multiple use tombs, with earlier interments swept to the sides. The numbers mentioned here exclusively refer to instances where the contexts indicated multiple interments deposited in a single event.

Elements in Religion and Violence

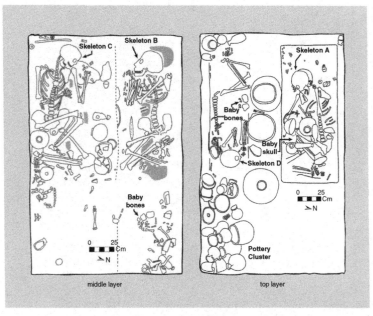

Figure 6 Tell Umm el-Marra Tomb 1, middle and top layers (after Schwartz et al. 2003: Figures 6 and 19. Courtesy of Glenn Schwartz).

men, women, and children, but very little indication of social status – other than in relation to an apparent main deceased. However, the remarkable preservation of some of these tombs (with many organic elements surviving, apparently even parts of a human brain in Tomb G1) reveals that also at Jericho, these burials represent sumptuous events. Large amounts of food in the form of joints of meat were found in all the tombs, and evidence of liquids was also present. The deliberate arrangement of the bodies similarly suggests an importance

Human Sacrifice

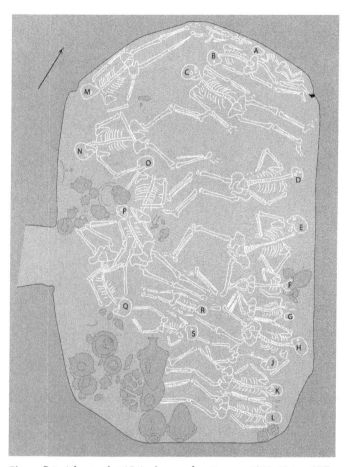

Figure 7 Jericho tomb P17 (redrawn after Kenyon 1964: Figure 175).

beyond the funeral process and the human participation. With the possible exception of P17 and P19 (where no 'main' burial was detected), the arrangement suggests retainer sacrifices, although the demographic, with a high number of children, could indicate that something else is also happening in these cases. P19 is unique in clearly revealing the violent cause of death, and the missing hands obviously tell a story that we are not quite able to decipher. Whether part of a ritual, an act of dishonour/punishment, or the result of conflict, the individuals were all honoured with a proper burial in a fairly well-equipped tomb.

Other Sacrificial Spaces

Human sacrifice may also have occurred outside mortuary contexts, as a few very diverse examples suggest.

At late third millennium Tell Brak, the large monumental complexes of Areas FS and SS appear to have been ritually closed, with deposits of complete donkeys; remains of a dog, pig, and gazelle; and jewellery, weapons, and tools. In Area FS, one deposit above the floor of an important room also included the remains of three incomplete human skeletons (all male), and in SS, human remains were found with and near one of the donkey skeletons (Oates et al. 2001: 42–43, 49–50; Molleson 2001). Along with the animals, which are quite carefully placed, these deposits all appear to be of a ritual nature related to the closure of the building, and both animals and humans may therefore represent sacrificial remains.[14]

Back at Tell Umm el-Marra, at a stage later than the third millennium mortuary complex, we find the so-called Monument 1 (c. 1900–1600 BCE – see Schwartz 2013: 508–513). The monument is a large circular structure covering

---

[14] Ritual deposits of human remains in a sacred area have also been recovered at Ebla, in the Sacred Area of Ishtar (Marchetti and Nigro 1997; Nigro 1998).

the area of the earlier tombs. A deep circular shaft had either been made with the structure or cut into it in its later phases. In it were 11 distinct layers of ritual deposits. The top ten layers consist of various animals, especially more equids and dogs, but also sheep/goats and two griffon vultures. The eleventh layer contained 13 humans, a dog, and birds. All the layers were distinct, but the ones with the humans were delimited by a line of stones both below and above. They were men, women, and children, and preliminary evidence of perimortem blunt force trauma on the skulls suggests they were killed by a blow to the head (Schwartz 2013: 512). It seems most likely that the deposits were made within a relatively short period, possibly even as a single event. The reason for this action remains obscure. The complete context is so far unique for the Near East, but its proximity to the earlier tombs and emphasis on equids and dogs suggests an attempt to connect with long-deceased ancestors. The choice of a deep shaft is reminiscent of the so-called *ábi* found at ancient Urkesh. The *ábi*, although from an earlier period, is believed to be a channel connecting to the underworld (c. 2300–2100 BCE – Kelly-Buccellati 2002; 2005). It is an over 6 m deep stone-built structure, and it also contained a large amount of ritual deposit of equids and puppies, along with pigs, sheep/goats, and birds (but no humans). The two structures may not be directly comparable (especially due to distance in time and the *ábi* being the focus of repeated ritual, while Shaft 1 may be a single deposit), but the shared features could indicate a desire to reach underworld entities through rituals that include sacrifice, be it ancestors, spirits, or deities.

A completely different scenario is found at the Late Bronze Age Amman Temple in Jordan (Wright 1966; Hennessy 1966, 1985). An isolated square stone structure is believed to be a temple, including a cella and an altar in the centre (Figure 8). A scatter of fragmented burnt human bones was found throughout the interior of the structure, especially in the cella, and outside near a feature called an 'incinerator'. The finds include many objects of

Elements in Religion and Violence

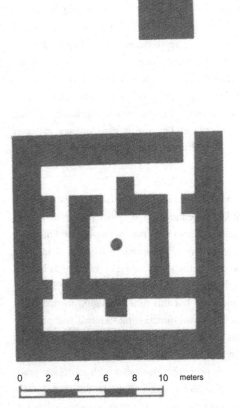

Figure 8 Amman Airport structure (after Herr 1983: 23. Courtesy of Larry G. Herr).

'foreign' origin (Hankey 1974a, 1974b), along with many lance or arrowheads, and cutting instruments (swords, daggers). The human bones are very fragmented, hampering identification, but appear to mostly belong to young individuals, although a 14–18 year old and a c. 40 year old are recorded. A minimum number of six individuals is represented. Not unexpectedly, the site is hugely controversial, with divergent interpretations not only of the human bones, but also the nature of the structure itself and its cultural affinities (e.g., Herr 1981, 1983). The idiosyncratic nature of the structure and its finds makes it difficult to interpret, but it does seem that some kind of ritual involving the burning of human bones took place. The site is most unusual whether mortuary or sacrificial activities (or both) took place.

Discussion

Outside mortuary contexts, human sacrifice in the Near East was rare and the possible examples we have are largely enigmatic. Whether or not they truly represent human sacrifices, elements of liminality, transformation, and memory are clear. Infants were placed in 'threshold' locations, incorporated into the architecture of the building, and thus perhaps remaining in memory as long as the building, while still being hidden from plain view. At Tell Brak, the complex is also committed to memory, but this time through a formal ritual that transforms it from functioning to non-functioning. Animal and possibly human sacrifices were part of this transformation, likely due to their connection with the complex when it was in use.

However, human sacrifice is primarily associated with mortuary practices. At Ur and Jericho, these appear to be mostly of the retainer type, while those at Tell Umm el-Marra suggest more complex rituals, possibly related to ancestors and commemoration rites. The human victims found in the Ur tombs were placed there during single events that most likely consisted of the royal persons' funerals (at Jericho, the status of the main deceased is more difficult to determine). Their simultaneous deposition is evidenced not only by the stratigraphy itself, but also by the overlapping of bodies in some instances. By all indications, these events must have been spectacular, with a flurry of colours and wealth combined with music, food, and a variety of 'actors'. Besides the preserved material in colours of gold, silver, copper, honey-brown carnelian, and lapis lazuli blue, Woolley mentions small pieces of bright red cloth (Woolley 1934: 239), revealing that this was at least one of the textile colours worn. Music had a very literal presence in the form of the lyres, and some of the 'ladies of the court' may also have been dancers, for which their elaborate jewellery and headdresses would have been particularly suitable. Food and drink were also found in the tombs, presumably for the next world rather than leftovers from the funeral feast, but the small bowls associated with many of these people suggest that they partook in some kind of consumption before their death, even if the bowls did not contain poison.

The social status of each retainer was signalled by the items with them and the context in which they were found. Even if we are not able to decode all the identifiers, we can with some certainty detect soldiers, musicians, animal attendants, and women whose social identity somehow revolves around their fine attire. Whether or not these people were substitutes – actors performing roles they had not actually fulfilled in life – is not known, but there is no immediate evidence to suggest they were.[15] Nor do we know if the king himself was a substitute, also sacrificed at this grand event, a phenomenon not unusual in myth and folklore (Frazer 1993: Ch. XXIV). There is again no reason to

---

[15] As shown by Vogel (2014) and Gansell (2007), diversity within the groups of women can also be detected by close examination of the items associated with them, thus establishing not only a more complex picture of the social identities present, but also of personal identities. This diversity lends support to the identity in death equalling that of life (i.e., not being substitutes).

believe this, and one might in such instance ask where the actual king was then buried.

No doubt the entire display would have been a sensational event, indeed not unlike a theatre performance, as one can imagine the procession of all these finely dressed people, soldiers, and animals, and the carrying of fine goods towards their final resting place. We do not know, of course, if such a procession in fact took place. The evidence for preservation suggests not. If treatments involving heating and mercury to preserve bodies for longer were carried out, this could almost certainly not have taken place at the tomb. This would greatly diminish the effect of the entire assemblage on the population at large, indicating that these displays were not in fact primarily intended for human viewing. Equally important, if not more so, were whichever supernatural beings were perceived to be able to appreciate it hidden in the ground. The manipulation of the arrangement postmortem testifies to this, as does the pure amount of wealth placed in the ground and thus removed from circulation. The diminished effect only applies if we assume that this was a spectacle primarily aimed at humans. Instead, whatever came next and whoever were able to see it may have been the main concern. Rather than a procession and a final resting place, we may see an assembly at their starting point, finding their place in the next life. In nearly every instance, mortuary and non-mortuary, there is a real concern with display and the arrangement of victims and related objects. Valuable goods (including humans and animals) are made unavailable for human consumption and placed in seemingly eternal exhibits.

3 Egypt

Large numbers of retainers were sacrificed at the burial of kings and other elite individuals in Early Dynastic Egypt. The practice appears to be largely

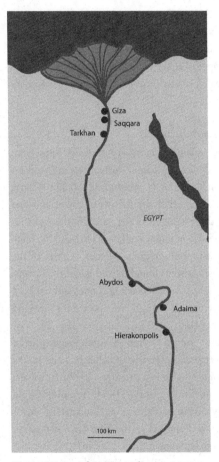

Figure 9 Map of Egypt with main sites mentioned in the text.

restricted to the First Dynasty (c. 2950–2775 BCE), with minor indications of earlier and later examples. The retainers are found associated with the tombs of royalty and possibly other elite individuals. However, other mortuary sacrifices, also of large numbers, appear at the enigmatic funerary enclosures in Abydos. Even before this time, recent work offers hints at ritual activity related to mortuary practices.

Earliest Indications

Early indications of human sacrifice related to mortuary practices come from Adaima and Hierakonpolis. At Predynastic Adaima, excavations in the West Cemetery have uncovered 349 tombs so far (Crubézy and Midant-Reynes 2005). Thirty-three of these were double burials, five were triple, and one contained six skeletons. Several of these were disturbed, but S55, the one with six skeletons, was not, and the bodies had in this case all been buried at the same time. They consisted of two adults and four children. Further, in three of the double burials (S11, S34, S24), incisions were found on the vertebrae of four individuals. These cutmarks are consistent with beheading (Ludes and Crubézy 2005). No parts of the bodies were removed, as might be expected if some kind of secondary mortuary ritual was involved.

At Hierakonpolis, evidence of trauma to human bones has also been detected in the form of lacerated vertebrae suggestive of beheading and marks on skulls that may come from scalping (Maish and Friedman 1999). However, the context of most of these in a non-elite cemetery (HK43) in mostly single burials does not currently strongly favour sacrifice as an explanation above other possibilities. More suggestive is Tomb 23 in the elite HK6 cemetery, along with its broader ritual setting (Friedman 2008a; 2008b) (Figure 10). Associated with this relatively large tomb was a deposit that included a cervical vertebra with cutmarks (Dougherty and Friedman 2008). The tomb itself contained at least 12 individuals, but it has not been possible to determine if

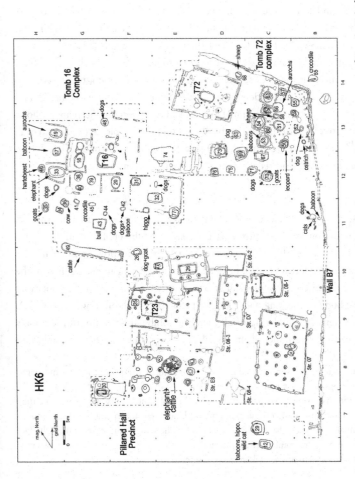

Figure 10 Hierakonpolis cemetery HK6 (cartography by Xavier Droux; courtesy of Renée Friedman).

they were buried simultaneously due to looting of the tomb. Tomb 23 is associated with mortuary temples and the nearby (slightly earlier) Tomb 16 complex, and both were surrounded by subsidiary tombs with an array of human and animal owners (Friedman 2011: 37–41). The animals are with some certainty believed to have followed their master in death (final meals were found partly in their stomachs, partly in their tombs), and it may be the same for some of the humans, whose selective placement and demographic are also suggestive. A new study identifies a third complex focussed on Tomb 72, also with subsidiary human and animal graves, and the demographic analysis shows clear selective patterns in the Tomb 23 and Tomb 72 complexes (Friedman et al. 2017).[16] The tombs are from the Naqada IC-IIB periods (mid to late fourth millennium BCE), so predating the Early Dynastic tombs at Abydos.

Early Dynastic Retainer Sacrifices

During the First Dynasty, and likely earlier, kings were buried at Abydos. These royal tombs[17] were primarily excavated by Flinders Petrie in the beginning of the twentieth century, but more recent excavations, particularly by German and American teams, have added greatly to our understanding of the site. The tombs consist of the subterranean structure with a main chamber that held the body of the king and associated chambers with offerings (Figure 11); despite extensive plundering of all the large tombs, the identity of the tomb's owner can be determined from inscribed objects found inside the tomb, and

---

[16] I am grateful to Renée Friedman for providing a pre-print copy of the paper presenting these new findings.

[17] The tombs at Abydos are usually considered royal tombs, but some believe that they were cenotaphs and that the actual tombs of kings were at Saqqara (see discussions in Hoffman 1984: 283–288; van Dijk 2008: 140). The disagreement stems from the fact that the Saqqara tombs are significantly larger, although not so if the funerary enclosures at Abydos are taken into consideration.

Elements in Religion and Violence

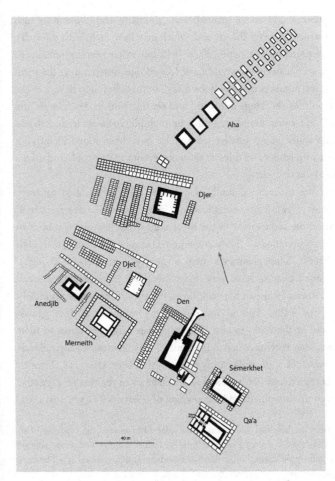

Figure 11 Abydos First Dynasty royal tombs (redrawn after Reisner 1936).

from stone stelae found above ground. Most probably, the tombs were also marked by a structure above the ground, which may have included a mortuary chapel (as suggested by O'Connor 2009: 154), but so far nothing remains to confirm what such a structure would have looked like. Surrounding the main tomb are varying numbers of small 'subsidiary' tombs believed to belong to the court and family of the king, following and serving him in death as in life. These tombs are often found in single or multiple rows with shared and relatively thin walls. Many smaller stone stelae have been found identifying the occupants with names and titles as various servants, craftspeople and others related to the king or court.[18]

Beside the main royal tombs at Abydos are the so-called funerary enclosures (Figure 12). These enigmatic and impressive structures were built 1.5 km north of the cemetery with the royal tombs, and have been subject to a number of interpretations.[19] They are large rectangular enclosures with high walls (the largest, Khasekhemwy's, may originally have been 11 m high). Remains of small chapels have now been identified as occupying a small space in the corner of some of the enclosures, but they otherwise seem mostly empty inside the walls. Around and outside the walls are retainer graves mirroring those at the main tombs, though perhaps slightly poorer in their contents. Each king may have had at least one of these enclosures corresponding to their tomb, although to date only those of Aha, Djer, Djet, and Merneith of the First Dynasty, and Peribsen and Khasekhemwy of the Second Dynasty, have been securely identified, and the owners of others are as yet unknown.

---

[18] In some earlier publications, these burials are referred to as *sati* (e.g., Reisner 1936; Hoffman 1984). *Sati* is a very particular form of Indian sacrifice where the wife of a deceased man would follow him in death at his funeral (often voluntarily). Thus it is not really appropriate for this material and also now very rarely used.

[19] For a short history of the excavations and theories concerning them, see O'Connor 2009: 159–162.

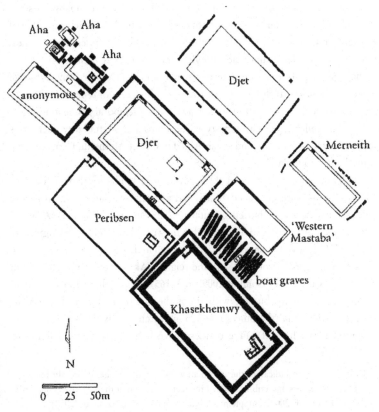

Figure 12 Abydos First and Second Dynasty funerary enclosures (after O'Connor 2009: Figure 88. Courtesy of David O'Connor).

The enclosures were clearly the focus of ritual activity, presumably in some way related to the ruler associated with each. Only the latest enclosure, that of Khasekhemwy's, the immense 'fort' also known as Shunet el Zebib, still stands, and there is evidence that each previous enclosure was deliberately razed, perhaps just before or when a new one was built (O'Connor 2009: 175–176; Bestock 2011: 141). If this is the case, the enclosures cannot represent places of long-term ancestor cult, but in some way served a temporary function.

The following First Dynasty royal tombs and/or funerary enclosures with retainers have been found so far: Aha, Djer, Djet, Merneith, Den, Anedjib, Semerkhet, and Qa'a.[20]

The tomb of Aha[21] had three rows of 36 tombs located to the east. The occupants were men aged 20–25, and a continuous layer of mud plaster suggests that they were buried simultaneously (van Dijk 2007: 138). A recent study of the remaining teeth indicates that they may have died by strangulation (Galvin 2005). Seven lions were also found each in their separate graves. Three funerary enclosures associated with the reign of Aha have been discovered in recent excavations (O'Connor 2009: 163–165). They all included a small number of subsidiary burials, with six at the largest enclosure, believed to belong to King Aha (the others may belong to elite individuals close to Aha rather than Aha himself). Five of these have been excavated and found to

[20] Unless otherwise indicated, the information on Abydos comes primarily from the excavation reports and publications of the teams excavating there (Petrie 1900, 1901, 1925; O'Connor 2009), supplemented by van Dijk's discussion (2008) and the detailed analysis by Reisner (1936). Cardinal point references use the local north.

[21] The area is also known as Cemetery B. The identification of a three-chambered tomb (B19, B15, B10) as belonging to Aha was made by Kaiser (1964: 96–102), and even earlier rulers may be associated with other tombs in the area as suggested by Petrie (1901) and more recent German excavations (see, e.g., Dreyer 1990; 2011). In earlier publications, Aha's tomb may be referred to as those of Narmer and his queens.

contain the remains of a young child, an adult man, and three adult women (Galvin 2005). The bones alone could not determine cause of death, but a plaster floor covering the enclosure also covers all the tombs, supporting the idea that the all the burials took place at the same time and could not have been 'added on' whenever an individual died naturally.

The number of small burials topped at the tomb and enclosure of the following ruler, King Djer. 326 small burials were found surrounding his tomb and extending to the north. As is usual, the burials mostly occur in large rectangular trenches divided into rows and single tombs by narrow internal walls, which would have made it difficult to close each tomb separately. This arrangement would also appear to support the simultaneous burial interpretation, but does not prove it on its own. Another supporting factor is that the stelae found in these tombs all carried female determinatives, which indicates a very select group – Petrie suggests the king's harem (1925: 3). Some of the burial clusters near Djer's tomb appear less organised and may represent tombs added where individuals died naturally: Reisner has carefully analysed in which tombs this may be the case (Reisner 2009: 117–121). The irregularities are in fact quite conspicuous from a look at the plans of both Djer and Djet's tombs, and the less neatly organised burials do seem to represent different activities not planned in advance.

Djer's funerary enclosure was surrounded by a similarly large number of tombs: 269. These are in neat double rows except for a few places with single rows and deliberate gaps in two corners. The tombs were again built in brick-lined trenches and divided by smaller walls, and re-excavation of some of the tombs during recent work has again revealed roofing that suggests all were closed at the same time (O'Connor 2009: 172–173). Several of these tombs led Petrie to conjecture that the victims had been killed by first being stunned and then buried alive due to the odd positions of some skeletons, which seem to indicate struggles (Petrie 1925: 7–8, pl. XIV).

Djer's successor, King Djet, had a tomb surrounded by 174 small burials. These are partly on the east and south sides of the tomb, but especially extend in clusters and rows to the north in more irregular patterns. Petrie records that the burial chambers were shut off by brickwork all around, and that a roof was placed permanently over everything (Petrie 1900: 10), again supporting simultaneous burial. This only seems to refer to the groups of small burials immediately to the east and south of the tomb, while the more irregular burials are recorded separately as 'Cemetery W'. The status of the latter are more difficult to determine, and Reisner believes that they may not all have been built at once based on internal differences in building techniques (Reisner 1936: 84–88). Djet's funerary enclosure was surrounded by 154 graves, including one with a dog in its own coffin.

The tomb of Queen Merneith (possibly the consort of Djet and mother of Den) has a central chamber with eight long chambers for offerings around it. Surrounding the main tomb is a neat, continuous single row of 41 small tombs, with a gap in the southwestern corner. Her funerary enclosure had 79 more irregularly placed tombs in a single line but built separately (note that the edge on the western side could not be found). Only male individuals are recorded, though few are identified (Petrie 1925: pl. XVIII).

No further funerary enclosures have been directly linked to First Dynasty rulers, but two others do belong to that period. One is the 'Western Mastaba', first discussed by Petrie, and connected with the exciting find in 1991 of 14 large boat tombs (O'Connor 2009: 183–194). The boat burials appear to belong to the same system as the subsidiary human burials, being placed in a row, in each their tomb next to an enclosure. Another enclosure found during the new excavations, just west of Aha's, also belongs to the First Dynasty, but is not yet further identified. No human subsidiary burials were found with it, but instead ten donkeys were discovered in three subsidiary graves (O'Connor 2009: 166).

The tomb of the next king belongs to Den. On the north and east sides, this tomb has triple rows of 121 small tombs, some of which may have been plastered over with the main tomb (Petrie 1901: 10). King Anedjib's tomb had 63 small tombs surrounding it, in a rather irregular pattern and with an additional branch added to the north. With Semerkhet's tomb, a change occurred in the relation between the main tomb and the subsidiary tombs. In this case, the 68 small tombs were part of the main tomb and apparently built directly with it. This means that the subsidiary burials must have all been covered at once and at the same time as the king himself. Among the humans found in these small tombs were two dwarves, identified both by their bones and by stelae.[22] Evidence of elaborate ritual was also found in front of the entrance to the tomb, where the sand was heavily saturated with ointment that could still be smelt in the whole chamber when Petrie excavated there (Petrie 1900: 14).

The last king of the First Dynasty was Qa'a. His tomb is immediately next to that of Semerkhet, and has a similar arrangement of small burials that are also directly part of the main structure. The 26 subsidiary burials surrounding the main chamber and storage chambers included at least one dwarf. Supporting the one-structure idea is Petrie's discovery of the lower levels of a wall that had crushed over several of the small graves due to being laid before the bricks were properly dried, just when the building was finished and presumably soon after the interment of the king (Petrie 1900: 14). This means that the subsidiary burials must have been placed during a very short period and all before the final closing off of the tomb.

---

[22] Dwarves have now also been identified in the earlier HK6 cemetery at Hierakonpolis (Friedman et al. 2017).

Subsidiary burials associated with First Dynasty royal tombs and funerary enclosures at Abydos

Deceased/site	Tomb (Umm el-Qaab)	Enclosure (North Cemetery)
Aha	36	6
Djer	326	269
Merneith	41	79
Den	121	not identified
Anedjib	63	not identified
Semerkhet	69	not identified
Qa'a	26	not identified

Note to table: The number of small tombs/subsidiary burials varies slightly in different publications (see especially Petrie 1900, Petrie 1925, Reisner 1936, O'Connor 2009). Significantly, while many of the small tombs certainly did hold humans, it is not clear if they *all* did so (partly due to plundering). Since the small burials were often similar to and functioned like the storage chambers, they were also at times used for inanimate objects, and we know that animals were also deposited in this manner.

The practice of subsidiary burials was not exclusive to Abydos in the First Dynasty, and in some cases retainer sacrifices may be involved.[23] At Saqqara, several mastabas dated to the First Dynasty include retainer burials similar to those at Abydos. Mastaba 3503, associated with Merneith, was surrounded by 20 subsidiary burials (Emery 1954: 133–138; 1961: 66, 137–139), although these all appear to have been built separately. Mastaba

[23] An alternative, though rather cumbersome interpretation for all the subsidiary burials is offered by Hikade and Roy (2015).

3504, associated with Djet, instead had three trenches (divided by cross walls as at Abydos) with rows of 62 subsidiary burials surrounding it (Emery 1954: 13, 1961: 71–73) (Figure 13). Similarly, Mastaba V at Giza had a single line of tombs on the west side, and separate subsidiary tombs surrounding the other three sides, 56 in total (Petrie 1907: 2–7, pls. II, IIIA, VI, VIA). At nearby Abu Roash, First Dynasty tombs with subsidiary burials have been discovered at Cemetery M (Tristant 2008). As an example, Mastaba 1 had seven subsidiary burials along one side and inside an enclosure wall, while Mastaba 7 had eight such burials. In the case of Mastaba 1, the burials were separate, and initially separately covered with layers of reed, sand, and bricks, but subsequently at least five (most likely all) were covered in a single layer of bricks, showing that all burials must have taken place when the mastaba was closed. Small stelae designating the owners were also found. At Mastaba 7, the burials were all in a single 14 m long trench, separated by bricks and all covered with a single roof. Finally, a few subsidiary burials of humans and animals were found at Mastabas 2038 and 2050 at Tarkhan (Petrie 1914).

After the end of the First Dynasty, evidence of human sacrifice becomes extremely scarce. The only possible indication comes from the funerary enclosure of Khasekhemwy at Abydos. Only the last two kings of the Second Dynasty (Peribsen and Khasekhemwy) were buried at Abydos. No subsidiary burials were found in Peribsen's tomb or funerary enclosure, nor in Khasekhemwy's funerary enclosure. Khasekhemwy's tomb had been heavily plundered and already cleared when Petrie excavated it (Petrie 1901: 12–13). The structure includes many parallel chambers suggestive of many burials, and Petrie found two skeletons, which he considered sacrificed retainers. The evidence here relies very much on the earlier examples and the layout of the tomb.

Human Sacrifice

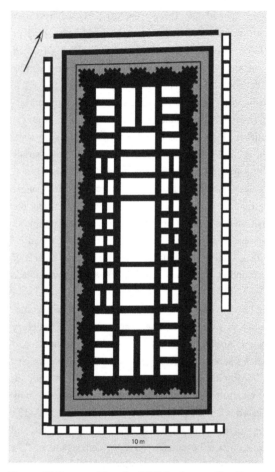

Figure 13 Saqqara Mastaba 3504 (redrawn after Emery 1961: Figure 34).

Iconography and Discussion

Egyptian iconography depicts its share of intra-human violence. Some imagery even depicts what appears to be highly ritualised violence, for example executions of prisoners of war following a battle. The famous Narmer Palette is one such example (see, e.g., O'Connor 2011). As Ellen Morris correctly observed, the distinction between ritual executions and sacrifice may be blurred (Morris 2014: 63–73), if not in some instances and cultures entirely non-existent.[24] Further, a few so-called labels from this early period include a depiction of a human figure with their hands apparently tied behind the back being stabbed in the chest by a kneeling figure who holds a bowl, presumably to catch the ensuing blood (Figure 14) (Crubézy and Midant-Reynes 2005: Figures 2 and 3). These tiny images are very revealing, and one important comment made by Bernadette Menu is that the victim is likely not a captive or slave, but probably a person of some importance, as he/ she is the same size as the standing figure (Menu 2005: 124), and not provided with any of the usual characteristic of a person being humiliated. Unfortunately, we do not know the relation to the archaeological data, and so far there is no evidence of stabbing in the skeletons studied or recorded by Petrie.

As far as recorded, the individuals buried with their king or queen were not dishonoured or treated differently than other deceased of their status.[25] Rather, an effort seems to have been made to represent them in death the same

---

[24] This is very relevant for some of the other examples discussed by Morris (as she notes) and here, but does not seem to apply to the Egyptian material, where at least the victims found archaeologically are unlikely to have been slaves or prisoners (see below). In accordance with the definition used here, if a ritual execution is done in the name of or to honour a supernatural entity, it is in fact a type of sacrifice.

[25] Although Petrie was careful to measure many skulls and long bones (note, e.g., 1925: 7–8 and pls. XX-XXI), the kind of careful osteological study sometimes undertaken today, as on the bones from Hierakonpolis and Adaima, was not typical when the royal tombs of Abydos were excavated in the early 20th century and consequently we only have limited data from the actual human bones.

Figure 14 Label from Saqqara, possible scene of sacrifice highlighted (redrawn after Crubezy & Midant-Reynes 2005: Figure 2).

as in life, sometimes buried with items showing their role and even with stelae providing personal names and titles. This strongly suggests that they really were understood as continuing to play the same role for their master in death, and that the symbolism does not extend beyond this. The tomb, tomb contents, and funerary enclosures must be seen as a complete assemblage, not just as a *representation* of the life and belongings of the main deceased but as their *actual* life and belongings, with all the varieties of goods and people that that entailed. Undoubtedly, the funeral and associated ritual and sacrifices constituted a great display,[26] but one that blurred the distinction between real and symbolic. As elsewhere, it could be argued that the courtiers and others buried in subsidiary graves were not the actual courtiers that had served the king/ queen in life, but rather substitutes (presumably slaves or others considered of lower value). The personal names on stelae, evidence of the bones (e.g., an actual dwarf directly linked to a stele naming a dwarf), and the evident importance of the person being able to perform the same role in death as in life (that is, have the same skills) speak against this interpretation. We thus appear to have a case where the sacrificial victims were *not* marginal individuals. There are no signs that these were slaves or captives, but instead integrated members of the royal court and extended workforce. How they died and whether or not they met their death willingly cannot at present be answered, but the proximity to the ruler and the respect shown could mean that it was considered an honour. If the data from outside Abydos is accepted, we can also conclude that mortuary human sacrifice was not a prerogative of the king or queen, although still only associated with individuals of high status.

4 China

Some of the largest numbers of human sacrifices recorded archaeologically come from Shang culture China. The ancient site of Yinxu (the modern city of Anyang in Henan Province) was the capital of the Shang state in the late period, c. 1250–1046 BCE. Extensive evidence of human sacrifice has been discovered

---

[26] On theatrical aspect of early mastabas, see Wengrow (2007).

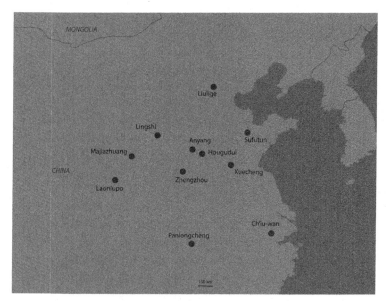

Figure 15 Map of China with main sites mentioned in the text.

at a royal cemetery at the site. The so-called Xibeigang cemetery contains thousands of 'burials' which are believed to be those of human sacrificial victims. The sacrifices appear to fall into two types: those accompanying royal burials, and simple single or multiple burials separate from the royal tombs.

Anyang Mortuary and Retainer Sacrifices

Xibeigang cemetery is divided into an eastern and a western section, and most of the large tombs are found in the western section (Figure 16). The royal tombs are large north-south oriented structures with a central chamber and four

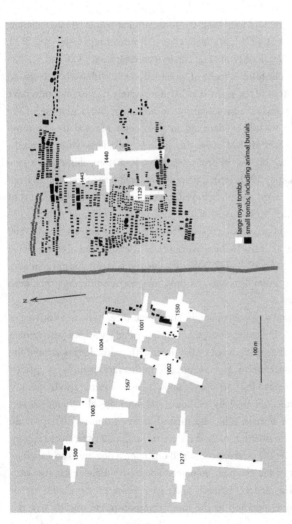

Figure 16 Anyang Xibeigang cemetery (redrawn after Li Chi 1977: 83, Figure 9).

sloping entrance corridors following the four cardinal points. As an example, the royal tomb HPKM 1004 has a main chamber measuring 10.80–15.90 x 13. 20–17.90 m, with a depth of 12 m. The corridors are between 13.80 and 31.40 m long (Li 1977: 85). The tomb is made of 'pounded' earth, with a wooden central chamber at the bottom of the main shaft. Unfortunately, the royal tombs have all been plundered several times, starting in antiquity, but a glimpse of the wealthy offerings can still be detected in places not reached by the tomb robbers. In the case of HPKM 1004, this includes two large bronze vessels, a cache of 360 bronze blades, 36 bronze spearheads, a stone chime and a jade (Li 1977: 88–90; Bagley 1999: 185). The only unlooted large tomb comes from the nearby Xiaotun area, a tomb believed to belong to Fu Hao, the consort of king Wu Ding. In it were found 468 bronze objects, 755 jade objects, 110 marble, turquoise and other stone objects, 564 carved bone objects, nearly 7000 cowrie shells, and at least 16 human sacrificial victims (see also extensive inventory list in Chang 1980: 237–238). As this tomb is significantly smaller than the Xibeigang examples, one can only imagine the offerings that were once placed in those.

The large tombs typically contain human sacrifices in three locations: in a sacrificial pit below the coffin of the main burial, called a *yaokeng* (also known as a waist pit, as it is near the waist of the deceased); on the ledges around the main wooden chamber, know as *ercengtai*; and in the various fill layers placed above the chamber and in the corridors/ramps. These locations also frequently contain other sacrifices, especially of dogs, and such are also found in less wealthy and smaller burials. The undisturbed areas of tomb M1001 provide good examples of the distribution and nature of the human sacrifices (Bagley 1999: 187–192). Here, the *yaokeng* contained one man, a dog and a so-called *ge* blade. Each corner of the chamber contained another two pits, each also with a man, a dog and a blade (Figure 17). At least some of these men are in a kneeling position as opposed to the more common prone one. Above the

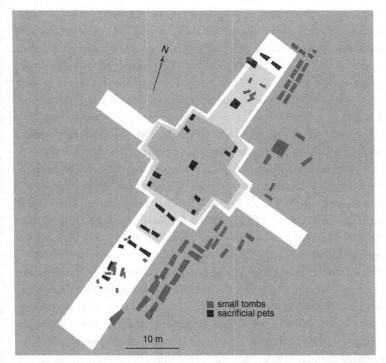

Figure 17 Anyang Xibeigang Tomb M1001 (redrawn after Tang 2004: Figure 7.3 and Bagley 1999: Figure 3.21).

chamber were another 12 victims, some in coffins and with a few offerings, some without either. As the corridors were filled up, more victims were included. The west corridor contained one complete adolescent, the east contained one headless skeleton, the east/west/north a total of 31 skulls, and the south corridor had 59 headless skeletons and 42 skulls – the skulls having been collected and placed in a higher layer than the bodies. They had been bound with their arms behind their back, and all but a few infants were adolescent males. Some of the smaller burials or pits are believed to belong directly to this tomb due to their proximity (37 in total, with humans and horses placed in them – Tang 2004: 124).

There are well over a thousand small tombs in Xibeigang, the majority found in the eastern section. Li records 1221 from the excavations in the 1930s alone, 1117 from the eastern section (1977: 82). They are also mostly oriented north-south, although a few are east-west (these are in fact later – Yang 1986: 53). They contain single or multiple skeletons (Figure 18). In the 1976 excavations, another 191 tombs or pits containing a total of over 1200 individuals were found (Bagley 1999: 193).[27] Essential for their interpretation as victims of sacrifice is the evidence of violence. Of the burials listed by Li, in 52 cases the skull had been separated from the body; in 209 cases only the skull was present; and in 192 cases only post-cranial remains were present (1977: 90).[28] There is also evidence of hands being bound behind the back. Of the 1976 finds, most displayed signs of violence, especially beheading, but also dismemberment, cutting in half and possibly even being buried alive. Most were young adult males, with only a few women and children, and were commonly neatly arranged in their final prone deposition. Decapitation thus seems one of the preferred methods of death, and the special emphasis on the head can also be detected in the way skulls and bodies are kept separate and the careful

---

[27] As of 2004, Tang notes that over 2200 sacrificial pits have been identified at Xibeigang, with a typical 3–10 individuals per pit (Tang 2004: 53).

[28] This led Li to conclude that all the small burials at Xibeigang were in fact human sacrifices. While this is a likely inference, unfortunately the material cannot at present substantiate it.

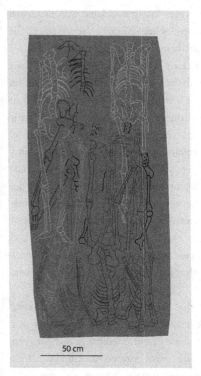

50 cm

Figure 18 Anyang Xibeigang small tomb with headless skeletons (redrawn after Chang 1980: Figure 37).

arrangement of, especially, skulls. It is possible that these victims were primarily slaves or prisoners of war, given their age and sex.

Given the different contexts and locations of the human sacrifices at Xibeigang, it does appear that we are dealing with at least two different types of sacrifice. The victims in the large tombs are closely associated with the actual death and funeral of a royal personage, where humans 'accompany' the deceased to the next world. The ritual here is comparable to what we see elsewhere, but we are at a loss as to exactly who the victims were and their relation to the deceased. Together with location, the evidence available on sex and age of the victims within these tombs suggests that those placed in the *yaokeng* and lower corners of the chamber possibly functioned as guards and/or as highly symbolic elements related to the Shang worldview. The Shang understood the world as square, oriented to the cardinal points and surrounding a core area (Keightley 1999: 269). It is surely not coincidental that this corresponds to the layout of the central chamber, with the 'core' wooden chamber inside, and the very deliberate placement of sacrifices in corners and the centre. Significantly, the victims in the corners of the M1001 chamber each had a bronze blade, while the central victim had a jade one (Bagley 1999: 189). The jade blade (broken, possibly deliberately) is not of practical use and may thus instead be related to the symbolic function served by the victim.

Equally interesting is the fact that the victim found in the *yaokeng* was often accompanied by a dog or even a dog on its own, suggesting that the role played by this element was to some extent interchangeable between man and dog – or perhaps that the two formed a kind of 'set'. The individuals placed on the *ercengtai* instead appear to constitute a more varied demographic and in some cases are shown more care in their funerary deposition: some were in coffins and given a small amount of grave goods. These victims could represent family or court members related to the daily life of the deceased. Finally, the victims placed above the chamber, in the corridors and fill layers, appear to be mostly young males and with more extensive mutilation of the bodies. The status and relation to the deceased in life of the individuals in the large tombs may not correspond to those in death. As elsewhere, all we can say is that they were *displayed* as having certain relations and performing certain roles, but the actual victims could be substitutes.

Aside from the main deceased, the individuals inside the large tombs were most likely part of ritual activity and sacrifice associated with the funeral, placed there immediately before and after the deceased. They belong to the same event, even if this event could have been prolonged over a more extended period (it is possible that the contents of the main chamber remained on display for a while before it and the corridors were filled in). In contrast, most of the small sacrificial tombs probably belong to later events. The tombs may in fact be divided into clusters or groups, each belonging to one ritual, as has been shown for the 1976 excavated tombs (Bagley 1999: 193). The proximity to the large tombs and general layout of Xibeigang suggests that the whole area was dedicated to a specific purpose, and this could well be the commemoration and worship of ancestors. In Shang religion, deceased (especially royal persons) could become ancestors and in a sense part of the 'pantheon' (see, e.g., Puett 2002). When this happened, the ancestor is given a name and a name day on which they are to be honoured. The small sacrificial tombs or tomb groups could thus correspond to the name days of ancestors, on which they receive sacrifices, among other things.

Human sacrifices are also found in other cemeteries at Anyang. Xibeigang appears to be the main royal cemetery, but a number of other cemeteries are found at the site, many of which are called lineage cemeteries because they are believed to belong to local extended family groups (Yang 1986: 56).[29] The deceased in these belong to all levels of society as far as

---

[29] It is estimated that a total of over 15,000 tombs have been excavated at Anyang to date (Campbell 2014: 141).

can be determined. In quite a few, there are examples of human sacrifice, usually in the larger tombs of each cemetery. At least six other cemeteries at Anyang have such sacrifices (Tang 2004: 48–53), including that at Houkang, where over 20 tombs had human victims, along with chariots and horses (Yang 1986: 58–59). The types of sacrifice mirror those of Xibeigang, albeit generally at a smaller scale. It is clear from these that although human sacrifice was rare or non-existent among the poorest of Anyang, it was by no means a privilege of the royal household, and certainly not an unusual occurrence.

Oracle Bone Inscriptions

Human sacrifice in the Shang period was in fact known or at least strongly suspected before it was discovered archaeologically. That is because it is mentioned in the so-called oracle bone inscriptions. These are inscriptions made on animal bones, typically turtle shell and the scapulae of cattle. They record various divinatory activities. Huge amounts of oracle bones have been found at Anyang, and these were sold as 'dragon bones' as a treatment for malaria long before excavations started at the site (Tang 2004: 2). The divinations were performed by the royal house at Yinxu and used to determine what the ancestors approved or did not approve of, including how many and what kinds of sacrifices should be performed (Keightley 1979/1980). One scholar studying the inscriptions has counted 14,197 human victims recorded on the bones (Shelach 1996: 13). Some of these appear to be Shang people, but a large group are individuals referred to as 'Qiang', a people as yet not well understood, but apparently an enemy to the Shang. They were captured during battle and at least in some instances used for sacrifice. This would explain the predominantly young male component of many of the contexts, and possibly also those where a weapon is found with the victim.

Construction Deposits

At Anyang, human sacrifices may also have taken place in connection with building activities or to help consecrate an area. Xiaotun is an area with buildings believed to be palaces and temples (Bagley 1999: 184, Tang 2004: 54–55). Numerous pits with humans, animals, and chariots were found associated with them, at least some of which can be connected with the construction of structures.[30] Both complete and beheaded humans were found. Tantalisingly, humans were also found associated with the foundations of a gate, with one left and one right of the gate, and one in the centre; a fourth was in front of the gate. Each skeleton was in a kneeling position and buried with a weapon (Li 1977: 106).

Evidence of rural practice of human sacrifice comes from the smaller site of Ch'iu-wan in the province of Kiangsu. Foundations of houses have been found belonging to the Neolithic and Shang periods. Contemporary with the Anyang occupation was an area designated as a place of sacrifice by the excavators (Bulling 1977). The area contained 20 human skeletons, two human skulls, and 12 dogs. The human skeletons that were well enough preserved to be identified included six males and four females, and were young to middle aged adults. They had all died a violent death and many had hands bound behind or in front. Some were found with holes in their skulls and stones next to them, leading to the suggestion that they may have been stoned to death. Their legs were bent as if kneeling or crouching. Most interestingly, all the heads had been turned to a focal point of several large *menhir*-type stones, interpreted as an altar.

---

[30] Others may instead belong to later rituals related to the function of the building (Yang 1986: 53–54). The area does also contain normal tombs. Some have human victims, including the tomb of Fu Hao (M5) and another large tomb likely with a female owner (M18) – see Chang 1986b: 70–71, Yang 1986: 54–55.

The skeletons were found in different layers and represent separate events. We are therefore here dealing with a continuous practice not of mass sacrifices as seen at Anyang, but a local small-scale ritual taking place on rare or special occasions. These sacrifices took place over some 200 years, apparently with dogs being more common in the earlier stages. There is no direct relation here to mortuary practices, but since the boundaries between spirits, ancestors, and deities in Shang and earlier religion were rather blurry, the entity represented by the altar may have a deeper association with ancestors. As at Anyang, Ch'iu-wan shows that human sacrifice was not confined to elite or royal activities and suggests more widespread and deeper religious practices that are not purely of ideological or political nature.

Outside Anyang

Further examples of human sacrifices in mortuary contexts roughly contemporary with Anyang and Xibeigang are reported at the sites of Sufutun, Liulige, Tianhu, Laoniupo, and Lingshi (Tang 2004: 56, Corba 1996: Figure 15). At Sufutun, tomb M7 contained three human sacrifices on the *ercengtai*, and tomb M1 had a total of 48 human victims (Figure 19), some headless and in layers in the south ramp along with five dogs; tomb M2 had a human skull in each corner of the shaft (Bagley 1999: 219–220, Chang 1980: 311, Campbell 2014: 144). At Laoniupo, 21 of 38 excavated tombs had sacrificial victims in them, mostly placed in *yaokeng* and niches – chariot and horse pits were also discovered (Campbell 2014: 154).

Human sacrifice was not a new phenomenon in Late Shang period Anyang. Nor did it end there. Earlier evidence comes from, e.g., Erligang horizon Zhengzhou, which includes a large deposit of skulls (some with brows sawed open) and pits with dogs and human skeletons (Chang 1980: 276, Bagley 1999: 166). From the same horizon come some large tombs found at Panlongcheng (Lijiazui), with human sacrifices in tomb M2 (Chang 1980:

Elements in Religion and Violence

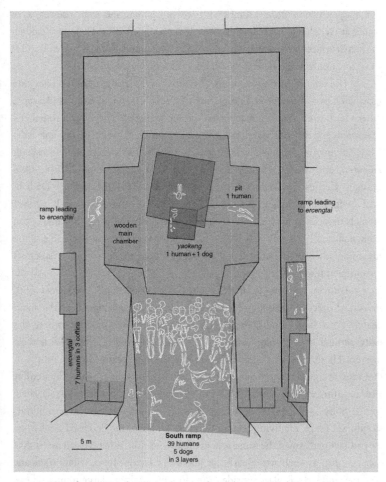

Figure 19 Sufutun Tomb M1 (redrawn after Chang 1980: Figure 85).

303, Bagley 1999: 170), and tombs with *yaokeng*, human and dog sacrifices, were found at Gaocheng Taxi (Bagley 1999: 178, Campbell 2014: 113). At Huanbei, human sacrifices are associated with walls and foundations (Campbell 2014: 111), a possible antecedent to the finds at Xiaotun.

Human sacrifices continue after the Late Shang period. They are especially associated with chariot burials (which occur already at Anyang, where both horses and humans make up a complete 'team' buried together). From a Western Zhou date (following the Late Shang) is a large tomb from Luiy Taiqinggong (Huaiyang) (Figure 20) with human victims in the *yaokeng*, *ercengtai*, and neatly arranged in the southern ramp (Campbell 2014: 148). Human victims are reported in large tombs at Fenghuangling, Dadian, Xuecheng (Shangdong), and Hougudui (Henan), and along with various animals associated with a ceremonial complex at Majiazhuang (Shaanxi) (von Falkenhausen 1999: 469, 502–506). These remains come from the middle of the first millennium BCE, but the contexts and similar treatment of victims suggests a continued tradition.

Human sacrifice in ancient China was particularly associated with mortuary practices and the ancestors. Its frequent appearance in the main chambers of large tombs illustrates a kind of retainer sacrifice, where the daily retinue of the ruler (or representations thereof) is buried with their master. These individuals generally receive a better treatment than others in that they are placed nearest their master and are sometimes placed in a coffin and/or afforded a few grave goods of their own. Where data is available, their demography is the most varied, consisting of men, women, and children. We do not know the living relation of these people to the deceased – whether they in fact performed the same role in life as in death. What we can say it that their staging as such was clearly an important factor. Just as important are the other individuals placed inside or in close proximity to large tombs. These seem to have a highly symbolic value. They are nearly always in liminal

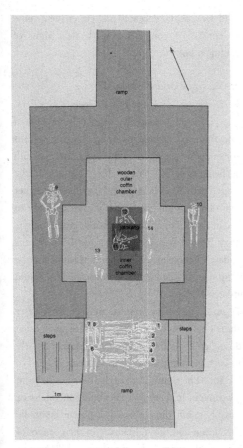

Figure 20 Luyi Taiqinggong, Chang Zi Kou tomb (redrawn after Campbell 2014: Figure 5.12).

locations – corridors, corners, and *between* the deceased and either the ground below or above. They largely consist of young men with clear signs of mutilation, but with carefully arranged bodies.

Discussion: Sacrifice and Ancestors

Deceased kings could become ancestors, and ancestors receive sacrifices. As sacrifice is a transformative act, it is aptly suitable as part of the process of making a king an ancestor. The funerary arrangements in the case of, for example, Xibeigang involved conspicuous display of a huge amount of wealth and power, the human sacrifices being only one part of this. The scale of the tombs and finds suggest a prolonged process. The repeated sacrifice of further individuals in groups at what were likely regular intervals served not only to honour what were now ancestors, but also to commemorate and remind people of the initial event. The ideology behind is made up of a web of religious beliefs, power, and political agendas. That the events were not peaceful and the victims not (at least not all) willing ones is graphically demonstrated by bound hands, and decapitated and mutilated bodies.

Human sacrifices outside purely mortuary contexts may in many cases also be related to ancestor worship. The sacrifices in these cases are again often placed in liminal spaces, with doors, gates, and foundations being particularly popular. A fascinating feature in both these and some mortuary cases is that of humans placed in a 'kneeling' position. The significance of this escapes us, but it is a deliberate and meaningful placement. It is not possible family members or retinue that are placed in this manner, but those serving a potent symbolic function – those at the gates in Xiaotun and the individuals in the corners of M1001 at Xibeigang come to mind. Anthropomorphic figurines in a 'kneeling-sitting' position may provide a clue. Li suggests that the posture is an ancient one related to proper ceremonial conduct, especially official audience of the ruler (Li 1977: 93). The connection between the figurines and the human victims is at present only tenuous, but offers a hint of the complex factors involved in these rituals.

5 Northern Europe

Bog Bodies

In bogs across Europe, human remains have been found ranging from isolated body parts to complete skeletons or bodies. Some of these have been interpreted as human sacrifices. The remains date from very early to modern times, and are concentrated especially in northern Europe, where the chemistry of the bogs is well suited for preservation.[31] Some of these finds are remarkable for their state of preservation. Bodies several thousand years old, with the complete skin, organs, and even brains have been found, along with remains of textiles and other personal items. Thus, the 'peaceful sleeping' facial expression of Tollund Man and 'look of horror' on Borremose Man have appealed to people everywhere, offering one of the most direct cases of a *face to face* contact with the past. The level of preservation has meant that in many cases, a long time passed before the finds were taken seriously, as dating techniques were still not well-developed and the bodies were assumed modern or at least not very old.

Prior to the twentieth century – and even some years into it – bog bodies were not considered particularly interesting, and often their fate after discovery in the bog is unknown; some were re-buried in the bog or re-interred in Christian cemeteries. In other cases, among other places, they were kept in museum stores and largely forgotten. The body of Huldremose Woman is

---

[31] The term 'bog' here covers different types of bogs, peats, fens, and mosses, which are distinguished by the way the peat is formed and stage of development (se e.g., Ó Floinn 1995a: 139; van der Sanden 1996: 21–37). Some types appear to be more conducive to preservation than others.

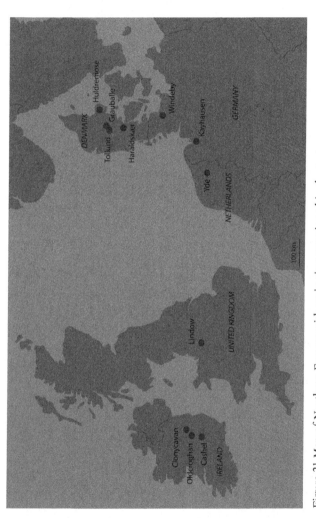

Figure 21 Map of Northern Europe with main sites mentioned in the text.

reported as kept under a desk in an institute at Copenhagen University until 1976 (Mannering et al. 2011: 37), around the time when research into bog bodies had really started gaining ground. Along with fascinating new discoveries, P.V. Glob's 1969 lively book *The Bog People* (originally published in Danish in 1965) helped popularise the topic and subsequent research.

Bog bodies are numerous, but exact numbers are not known. In his comprehensive survey of European bog bodies from 1965, Alfred Dieck records nearly 700 examples (broadly defined and including skeletal remains and isolated body parts). Many come from Denmark, Germany, the Netherlands, Ireland, and Britain. Dieck's catalogue includes so-called paper-bodies, that is, finds only known from local newspapers or even word of mouth, without any extant physical remains. Subsequent finds have been made, but the catalogue is still one of the most comprehensive and provides a good overview. It does have some problems of authenticity, however.[32] More recent catalogues and distribution maps can be found in Briggs and Turner 1986 (Britain and Ireland), Turner 1995 (Britain), Ó Floinn 1995b (Ireland), Fischer 1980b (Denmark distribution map), van der Sanden 1995 (Netherlands), Lund 1976 (Europe distribution map), and van der Sanden 1996 (Europe distribution map, 196–197).

The cases listed in these catalogues include all time periods and circum-stances; the ones believed to represent human sacrifices mostly belong to a limited period from roughly 500 BCE – 1 BCE, the first part of the Early Iron Age (in Denmark also known as the pre-Roman or Celtic Iron Age), but there are also earlier cases from Ireland and Denmark. Unfortunately, many bog bodies have not been securely dated due to the find circumstances, and

---

[32] Serious doubt has now been cast on the legitimacy of some of Dieck's entries and sources (van der Sanden 1995: 152; Lund 2002: 36) and, without verification, especially the paper bodies should be approached very carefully.

much knowledge has likely been lost in this manner. However, the few bodies that have been preserved and researched carefully provide a wealth of information, along with as many questions.

The bodies discussed here stand out because of their mode of deposition and strong evidence of violent deaths. During this period, cremation was the norm. Individuals treated differently from this norm likely had a special role, in life or in death, and as such, sacrifice may apply to at least some of the bog bodies from this period. The evidence for violence is clear in a good few examples, as we will see, but the big question surrounding the bog bodies is whether or not we are dealing with religious killings – human sacrifices. There are no direct contemporary written records from the areas with the bog bodies, so we rely on a combination of Roman sources, iconography, and archaeological material for indications of the religions and sacred life of the various relevant cultural groups.

Bog Body Problems

Certain caveats hamper the interpretation of finds from bogs. The most important of these is the issue of dating the finds. Finds associated with bog bodies can in some cases be roughly dated on stylistic grounds. Thus, a body from Bocksten Bog in Sweden could be dated to the fourteenth century CE based on his clothes (Glob 1969: 148–149). Many bog bodies have few or no associated finds, and the few finds are rarely chronologically diagnostic. This means a heavy reliance on radiocarbon dating. Radiocarbon dating has been done both on soft tissue from the bodies, and from the surrounding peat, but both of these come with serious problems. The dating of human tissue using ^{14}C is still not entirely understood, and it seems likely that the older water from the bog can contaminate it (Tauber 1980; Briggs 1995: 172). Radiocarbon dating of peat is in itself not as problematic; doubts arise when making precise associations between the peat and the body – the peat surrounding the body can be very active, and need not necessarily correspond to the deposition of the body (Briggs 1995: 172–173). An excellent example of these problems is represented by Lindow Man, where both the peat and the human tissue were dated and provided significant discrepancies (Joy 2009: 23).

Many bodies are reported as naked or nearly naked. This is an important interpretative factor. But were they really naked? It is possible that in some instances, certain types of textiles were not preserved in the bog even though human tissue was. As this is a case of absence, it generally cannot be proven one way or the other, but the evidence from Huldremose Woman gives cause for caution. Aside from the clothes found with her, several textile marks were on her skin, and one of these does not correspond to any of the items found, but to an unpreserved garment, probably an under-garment of a kind of plant fibre (Mannering et al. 2011: 41–42). The context of Tollund Man, with merely a belt and a cap, springs to mind as particularly odd, and could perhaps be explained by unpreserved garments. That is not to say that all the bodies found naked in fact had been deposited with clothes, but that arguments based purely on nakedness must be made with care.

Interpretations

The concept of 'bog bodies' is an artificial category, at least in terms of its cultural significance. The main common factor is merely the find spots: bogs (Lund aptly calls it a 'muddy' category – Lund 2002: 83). Beside that, they come from all periods from the Neolithic to modern times and point to a variety of events, many of which we are unable to reconstruct with much detail. Nevertheless, many of the bodies belonging to the last 500 years BCE in northern Europe have similar features and appear to be part of a shared practice that may have involved sacrifice. This 'group' may not be complete or even representative. Bodies could have been deposited in a similar manner, but in an environment that does not have the same preservative qualities as bogs. Keeping this in mind, the examples that do survive often show signs of trauma and/or an unnatural death by human hands. Binding, stabbing, hanging, strangulation, decapitation, blows to the head, and throat cutting are some of the traumas suffered. Although not clear in all individual cases, the presence and use of violence on bog bodies is conspicuous. The question is under what circumstances it was carried out.

The interpretations are almost as varied as the bodies themselves. Apart from being seen as victims of sacrifice, some bodies are thought to represent executed criminals (possibly understood as ritual or sacred executions), victims of crime, accidents, marginal individuals perceived as dangerous to the group of which they were part, and therefore forcibly removed (a role approximating that of witches), and in a few cases, as 'normal' interments.[33] Most commentators agree that not a single explanation can cover all the bodies from even this limited time period, and this is indeed important to emphasise. Each case must be evaluated individually, and seen in the broader cultural context of the period. Each interpretation is possible for some cases, based on the available evidence. This is more than anything a testament to the fragmentary and incomplete nature of the data at hand.

Denmark

One of the earliest examples from the period of interest here also has a characteristic modern story. 'Queen Gunhild' was found in 1834 in Haraldskær Bog, near Vejle in eastern Jutland.[34] At the time of the discovery,

---

[33] Reviews of the different interpretations can be found in van der Sanden (1996: 166–177). Suicide (without Christian connotations of sin) has also been noted as an option (e.g., Lund 2002: 51), but is rarely considered a good explanation for the kinds of trauma found.

[34] Other finds from Denmark of interest here include the bodies from Borremose (Thorvildsen 1953). Finds dating to earlier periods with possible evidence for sacrifice include those from Sigersdal (Early Neolithic, Bennike and Ebbesen 1986;

a well-respected historian argued that the woman was in fact the wife of King Harald Bluetooth. The legend goes that the king had persuaded the queen of Norway to come to Denmark to marry him, but when she arrived, he instead drowned her in a bog (Hvass 1998: 9–12). The body was later ^{14}C dated to 490 BCE, and so of course could not have been the Norwegian queen, but the name sticks and the body is still commonly known by her royal name ('Haraldskær Woman' is also used). She was about 40 years old when she died. A leather cape and other textiles were associated with her, but it is unclear if they were on top of or near her, or if she had been wearing them (Hvass 1998: 10–11, 14). She appears to have been nailed to the ground of the bog with poles and stakes, which have left deep grooves on her arms and legs. Another groove in her neck may point to strangulation as the cause of death. Intriguingly, new research shows that shortly before her death, she undertook a substantial journey (Frei et al. 2015b). It is not yet possible to determine how this journey relates to her final fate, but similar results have been reached for the Bronze Age burial of the Egtved Girl (Frei et al. 2015a), who appears to represent a 'normal' burial (she was in a coffin with grave goods), yet the burnt bones of a child were found with her.

Two of the most famous and evocative bog bodies were found less than 20 km apart in eastern Jutland, Denmark. They are known as Tollund Man and Grauballe Man. Tollund Man was found in 1950 in a bog near Tollund (Glob 1969: 18–36; Tauber 1980: 77; Nielsen 2014). Tollund Man is an adult male about 30 years old (Figures 22 and 23). The body was complete and placed on the side with the legs bent upwards. It was found with a pointed skin cap, a hide belt, and a leather rope around the neck. Stubble is today visible, but this is

Andersen 1987), Porsmose (Neolithic, Becker 1952); Bolkilde (Early Neolithic, Bennike et al. 1986), Stenstrup (Neolithic, Bennike and Ebbesen 1985) and Egtved (Bronze Age, Frei et al. 2015a).

probably due to shrinkage of the skin – at death, Tollund Man was likely shaved and with short-cropped hair. His fingernails were well-kept, and the relatively fine skin on his hands may indicate a lack of hard manual labour.[35] His eyes and mouth were closed, giving the impression of peace, but the cause of death has been determined as hanging, without a severe free fall. Tollund Man has most recently been dated to c. 397–263 BCE (Nielsen 2014; earlier results of c. 220 BCE in Tauber 1980: 77, Fischer 1980b: 29). He was placed in the bog before rigour mortis set in (Lund 2002: 51). Tollund Man's cause of death, combined with the body position, which appears to reflect a careful and respectful place-ment by his survivors, rules out accident and makes execution unlikely. There are no signs of disease or anything else that might point to a marginal individual; the well-kept nails support the idea of a fairly well off person.

Grauballe Man was found only two years after Tollund Man in Nebelgård Bog (Glob 1969: 37–62; Asingh and Lynnerup 2007) and is dated to 400–200 BCE (Heinemeier and Asingh 2007). He was partly damaged by the peat diggers, but not extensively. Grauballe Man was about 30 years old when he died, and he was found completely naked and with a deep cut across his throat, presumed to be the cause of death (Gregersen et al. 2007). He had also received a blow to his forehead, and his left shin had suffered a trauma, the former perhaps a postmortem injury. Recently, it has been suggested that his throat injury could instead have come from a failed rescue attempt, the marks on the neck instead being a 'worn burn-mark' from the rescue rope/line around his neck (Briggs 1995: 177). Disregarding the unlikeliness of this method of rescue (even in desperation), Grauballe Man would have had to have fallen into

---

[35] See however Fischer, who observes that only the inner layer of skin is commonly preserved on bog bodies, the outer layer having dissolved after long immersion in water (Fischer 1980b: 26–29). This makes inferences concerning labour patterns based on the condition of the skin less persuasive.

Figure 22 Tollund Man (Courtesy of Silkeborg Museum).

the bog naked and the unsuccessful rescuers somehow retrieved their rope (unless, of course, his clothes and the rope all disintegrated in the bog).

About 50 m from Tollund Man, a female bog body was found in 1938, known as Elling Girl (Fischer 1980b: 12–25; Tauber 1980: 77–78; Nielsen 2014). An animal hide had been wrapped around her legs, meaning she was initially mistaken for a deer, and damage was caused to the body (Figure 24). The body is that of a female[36] aged 25–30, with an elaborate hairstyle created from her long hair. A leather rope with hairs from her body still attached was found near her and matches a groove in the back of the neck, providing

---

[36] Doubt has been cast on the sex of the body, as this was first determined purely on the grounds of her long hair, but subsequent studies have identified it as almost certainly female (Gregersen 1980; Langfeldt and Raahede 1980; Philipsen 1980).

Figure 23 Tollund Man (Courtesy of National Museum of Denmark).

a strong clue to the cause of death. Elling Girl is dated to 335–263 BCE, making her at least potentially contemporary with Tollund Man. The deerskin wrapped around Elling Girl's legs strongly suggests that she was deliberately placed in the bog. The cause of death is conjectural, and the

Figure 24 Elling Girl (Courtesy of National Museum of Denmark).

case for it not being a natural interment is largely based on knowledge of common burial practices at the time.

Possibly contemporary is the Huldremose Woman, dated to 350–41 BCE (Figure 25) (Tauber 1980: 76). Her hair had been cut short and placed next to the body, and a stake had been placed over her body, presumably to stabilise

Figure 25 Huldremose Woman (Courtesy of National Museum of Denmark).

its position. The woman had received stab wounds on arms, legs and one foot; her left arm had been fixed to her body, and her right arm cut off in ancient times (Brothwell et al. 1990). Unusually, the roughly 40 year old woman was wearing a full set of clothes consisting of two skin capes (one with a sewn-in 'pocket' containing a comb, hairband, and leather cord wrapped in the skin of an animal bladder), a woollen skirt, a woollen scarf, and an inner garment which has not survived but left marks on the skin of the woman. Associated with the scarf was a wool cord with two amber beads and a bird bone pin. One of her fingers had the imprint of a ring (Mannering et al. 2011: 35, Figure 1). The ultimate cause of her death is unknown, but the violence inflicted on her limbs strongly suggest it was not accidental. The absence of a finger ring could suggest a robbing, but it is not known when the ring was removed, and the quantity and quality of the rest of her finds are remarkable.

The Netherlands and Germany

Indications of the cause of death from Dutch bog bodies have only been identified in a few cases.[37]

One is the girl from Yde, who was only 16 years old when she died around 1 CE (van der Sanden 1995: 83, 91, 131, 135, 157, 161). She was found in 1897, with remains of a woollen cape and long hair, coloured red by the bog, but probably originally blond. Around her neck was the woollen band with which she had been strangled. It had been wound around her neck three times, and then tied in a knot that is still visible near her left ear. She suffered from a condition called idiopathic scoliosis, which may have had a visible physical deformity or disability. The knotted band wound several times around her neck proves that she did not die by accident and that the band cannot come from rescue attempts. Her possible physical deformity could support either the execution/crime or the sacrifice interpretations.

---

[37] The so-called Weerdinge bodies of two men also had signs of violence possibly related to cause of death (van der Sanden 1996: 102). An older, Bronze Age bog body from the Netherlands is the Ascbroeken Man, who was found with stakes over his body in Bourtanger Moor in 1931 (van der Sanden 1996: 78–79).

Some of the most unusual and graphic bog bodies come from Germany.[38] The so-called Kayhausen Boy is one example (Hayen 1964). At the age of 7.5, the young boy was placed in a bog in northwestern Germany. He had been elaborately bound with a piece of textile around the neck and in a line down the front of his body, between his legs and around the back of his body back up to the neck (Figure 26). The hands were bound on the back in the process, and his ankles were also tied together. This arrangement meant that he could have been easily bundled up and carried. The boy had been stabbed three times in the neck and once in the left arm. In life, the boy had a serious hip joint problem which would have made walking extremely difficult. The find is dated to 364–50 BCE.

'Windeby Girl' (or 'Windeby I') was found in 1952, also in northwestern Germany and dated to around 1 CE (Gebühr 1979; Grüner 1979; van der Sanden 1996: 81, 97–98, 112, 164–165, 169).[39] Placed in an old peat digging, the body was naked except for a small cape around the shoulders. The hair had been cut short on one side of the head only, and around the head and face was a tightly bound hair net. This is commonly reconstructed as a blindfold, but may also have been placed over the mouth (it was found fairly tight over the nose). The cause of death is not known, but a large stone was at her hip, assumed to hold the body down.

Ireland

Ireland presents the most recent finds of bog bodies, with Clonycavan Man and Oldcroghan Man found in 2003 and Cashel Man in 2011 (Kelly 2006; 2012a;

---

[38] Not discussed here, but of interest are Dätgen Man (Struve 1967; Aletsee 1967), and the bodies from Grosses Moor/Hunteburg (van der Sanden 1996: 102).

[39] There is some doubt about the sex of this body, which may not be female, as first assumed (Lund 2002: 62).

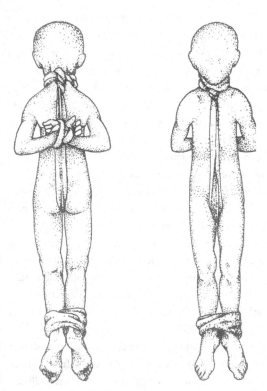

Figure 26 Kayhausen Boy (after van der Sanden 1996: 93. Courtesy of Wijnand van der Sanden).

2012b). Clonycavan Man was found in Co. Meath during peat digging, and was damaged from the waist down by the peat digging machine. He was killed by a series of blows to the head and chest by an edged weapon, possibly an axe, and a 40 cm long cut in his abdomen could indicate disembowelment. The digging of a bog drain led to the discovery of Oldcroghan Man, whose severed torso had been stabbed in the chest and decapitated in antiquity. Intriguingly, withies had been inserted into the cuts. Clonycavan Man has been dated to 392–201 BCE, and Oldcroghan 362–175 BCE. In both cases, there are suggestions that they were not low status individuals: Clonycavan Man had a distinctive hair-style which used a kind of gel (resin) originating in France or Spain, and Oldcroghan Man had carefully manicured fingernails and absence of wear on the hands. Both men have had their nipples cut, although it cannot be deter-mined whether this was pre- or postmortem.

Cashel Man not only represents the most recent discovery, he may also be the oldest 'real' bog body known from Ireland, dated to the Early Bronze Age, about 2000 BCE (Kelly 2012b).[40] He was heavily damaged by the peat digging machine, but it was still possible to identify two breaks in his spine and cuts to the back, perhaps caused by an axe. Two hazel stakes had been placed at angles over the head of the body, marking the deposition. Gallagh Man, closer in date to the former two Irish bog bodies (first century BCE), also had a stake or wooden post placed on either side, and was found only with a leather cape. He may have been strangled with the "band of sally rods" found around his neck (Ó Floinn 1995a: 139; 1995b: 226 Ga1).

Kelly interprets these remains, along with a number of other Irish bog bodies, as sacrificial victims. All three men were placed on Irish county borders, and several others are noted in similar locations (Kelly 2012a: 237). Kelly argues that the Irish county borders may well have ancient origins, and that the sacrifices are related to kingship (with suckling of nipple being associated with kings), inauguration, and the marking of borders. The liminality of bogs is in this case doubled, being both physically in

---

[40] Another Irish bog body dates from the Middle Bronze Age, around 1431–1291 BCE (Derrycashel Man from Co. Roscommon – Kelly 2012b: 10).

between territories and geologically between land and water. Such an interpretation is appealing, especially considering the lack of knowledge surrounding the broader context of bog bodies, but does require a leap beyond the archaeological evidence alone. What seems fairly certain in these cases is the violence related to death, and the type of violence, placement of the bodies, and indications of status suggest that we are not here dealing with simple crimes, executions, or marginal individuals.

Discussion

The bog bodies discussed here could represent human sacrifices. This is by no means beyond doubt, and it should be emphasised that many other cases may not as easily be so interpreted. For obvious reasons, the examples chosen here are ones where the sacrifice interpretation fits fairly well. Unfortunately, if these were indeed sacrifices, we are left with very little information about the circumstances and occasions on which they took place. Apparently, the sacrificial victim could be male or female (although outside Denmark, male bodies predominate), child or adult, diseased or healthy, and does not seem limited to individuals of low status. Neatly kept fingernails, possibly lack of signs of hard manual labour and items presumably of some value indicate the opposite. For the Irish bodies, it is even suggested that they may have been deposed kings (Kelly 2012a: 239). Individuals with physical impairment could have been low status, but it is also possible that their impairment made them especially suitable for sacrifice, perceived as a supernatural feature.

From the archaeological evidence, we know even less about who performed the ritual or occasions on which it was required. A distinction between sacrifice and ritual execution can be very difficult to determine in the given archaeological evidence, and such a distinction might not even be relevant to ancient conditions.[41] Victims of ritual execution might not have been treated with as much respect as those of sacrifice, but this is purely conjectural, and we do not know that either type demanded special honour after their death.

If we assume that bogs were the only or prime location where sacrifices took place, then this is certainly a significant aspect. The bodies constitute remarkable and deliberate placements in a preservative environment. Discoveries of 'bog butter' in Irish bogs indicate knowledge of the bog's qualities at least in that area (e.g., Earwood 1997), and this may also have been noticed during ancient peat digging. Although Glob's theory of a late winter fertility rite is not borne out by the evidence, there is indirect support for the depositions taking place only in colder seasons. For a body to be preserved, it has to be immersed in the bog fairly quickly and at a temperature below 4°C (Gregersen 1980: 54–55). The use of stakes and branches to hold bodies down or in place might be seen in this context as a means to ensure that the body remained immersed and thus preserved.[42] It is also striking that quite a few of the bodies (this is believed for, e.g., the Tollund Man, Grauballe Man, Windeby I, Dätgen Man, and Borremose bodies) were placed in ancient peat diggings or natural hollows.

Indirect evidence for the sacrifice interpretation comes from the idea of the bog as a sacred, mystical, and liminal place (see also Asingh 2007). This is based more on folklore and Roman writings than archaeological material (Ross 1986; Turner 1986; Magilton 1995; Aldhouse Green 2001). But what we do

---

[41] In the theory of sacrifice as proposed by René Girard, sacrifice essentially *is* ritual execution, with the victim perceived as guilty (Girard 1986; 2005).

[42] In the interpretation of some bog bodies as witches, the stakes were used to prevent the person from 'walking again' (Lund 2002: 84; Gebühr 1979: 97). If this were the case, it would seem strange to place them in a preservative environment.

know is that bogs are indeed treacherous places, environments that easily lend themselves to marginality and liminality, being outside settlements and neither land nor water. Some archaeological support for the idea of bogs as sacred is found in non-human objects placed as some kind of votive offerings. These have been documented in many bogs from at least as early as the Bronze Age, and show that some bogs were considered suitable for sacred depositions (see, e.g., Randsborg 1995 for the Iron Age deposition of a complete boat and army equipment, also Simonsen 1953; Fischer 1980b: Figure 19 for distribution map of Danish finds). While this does not suggest the equal sanctity of all objects found in all bogs, it offers a view of the human relationship with bogs in ancient times. We also know that from very ancient times, bogs were dug for peat as spades (Fischer 1980b: 11) and peat diggings have been discovered. The exact extent of this activity is not known, but it is not impossible that it was considered appropriate to offer sacrifices in return for the peat taken. Fischer's observation that there seems to be some correspondence between deposition of ceramic vessels in bogs, human bodies, and peat digging activity in Denmark is revealing. As he suggests, the sacrifices may then be related to this activity, functioning as thank offerings (Fischer 1980b: 39–41) occurring some time after an area had been used for peat digging.

6 Mesoamerica

Ancient Mesoamerican cultures are infamous for mass and gruesome human sacrifices, with images of long lines of human victims having their hearts torn out and their bloody bodies thrown down the front of pyramidal temples. Large crowds watch, partly terrified, partly cheering on the action. Such scenarios have been presented to the public through Hollywood movies and brought down to us through the writings of the Spanish conquerors. The Aztecs in

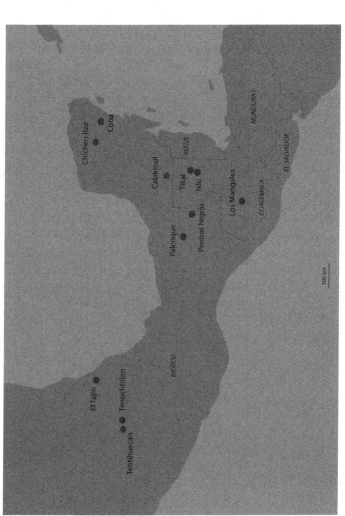

Figure 27 Map of Mesoamerica with main sites mentioned in the text.

particular are recorded as practicing these kinds of spectacular events. The sensational descriptions are in part supported by archaeological remains and images created by the Aztecs themselves, as the limited material from their capital city Tenochtitlan reveals.[43]

Mesoamerica (modern Mexico, Belize, Guatemala, Honduras, and El Salvador) consisted of a variety of 'cultural' groups such as the Olmecs, Zapotecs, Maya, Teotihuacanos, Toltecs, and Aztecs. Some of these groups are contemporary, while others only appear earlier or later in prehistory. The groups interacted through trade, warfare, and inter-marriage, and to some extent also shared, were influenced by, and adapted each other's religious views and ideologies. The practice of human sacrifice may thus have occurred in many, if not all, of the groups in a range of forms and expressions. These forms also changed over time. The famous mass sacrifices, for example, seem to have been a feature largely confined to the Late Postclassic period, perhaps especially influenced by, and partly creating, Aztec ideology (e.g., Demarest 1984). These are important distinctions to keep in mind when reading what follows, where material coming from different cultures and periods is some-times brought together.

Due to the unusual conjunction of archaeological contexts, osteological and iconographic studies, the advancements in the decipherment of Mayan glyphs (Schele and Miller 1992: 323–328), and extensive colonial records,[44] we

---

[43] Tenochtitlan is now below Mexico City, and therefore only very limited excavations have been possible. Part of an important structure has been found (Templo Mayor) which includes a construction deposit with the bones of over 40 children, and the dramatic pieces of art include a huge relief with a dismembered goddess and a *chacmool* on top of the pyramid (see especially Matos Moctezuma 1988).

[44] Although the focus here is on archaeology, readers may be interested in the writings of Bernal Díaz del Castillo, Diego de Landa, Bernardino de Sahagún, and Toribio de Benavente (Motolinía). The sources of the conquerors are extremely informative

probably know more about human sacrifice in Mesoamerica than anywhere else. We have good evidence for at least some types of sacrifice, sacrificial events, victims, and methods, even if these are neither exclusive nor apply to all regions and periods. Events that involved human sacrifice include elaborate accession rituals, construction and termination rituals, the famous ball games, and the deaths of high-ranking individuals. The discussion below focuses on selected elements and types of sacrifice, but in fact few contexts are confined to only one of these types.

Construction Sacrifice

The site of Teotihuacan lies 40 km northeast of Mexico City. It was founded by 300 BCE, and flourished until 700–800 CE (later it was occupied by the Aztecs). It is believed to be a major ceremonial centre, with its famous Sun and Moon pyramids, Avenue of the Dead and the Ciudadela with the Feathered Serpent Pyramid, and some 600 smaller pyramids (Figure 28). Residential areas have also been identified. Remains of human sacrifices have been identified in the Feathered Serpent Pyramid and the Moon Pyramid.[45]

In the Moon Pyramid, human sacrifices were associated with new construction phases (Figure 29). Seven building stages were identified, and beginning with the fourth stage, each new one was accompanied by human sacrifices, with a total of at least 37 human victims (Spence and Pereira 2007: 147; Sugiyama and Cabrero Castro 2006; Sugiyama and López Luján 2006). At the construction of the phase 4 building, c. 250 CE, a chamber was located at

(and make for very graphic reading), when used with caution, since they naturally reflect the mindset of their writers who were after all there to conquer and convert.

[45] Sacrifices were also found associated with the Pyramid of the Sun, a child aged around six having been placed in each corner (Batres 1906: 22); more may exist (Millon 1992: 395, n. 67).

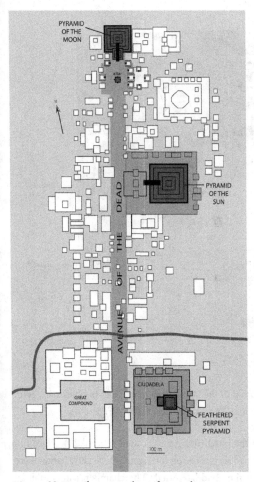

Figure 28 Teotihuacan, plan of area along Avenue of the Dead.

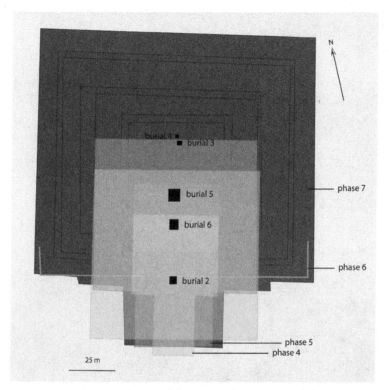

Figure 29 Teotihuacan Pyramid of the Moon, schematic plan of phases 4–7 with burials (redrawn after Sugiyama and Lopéz Lujan 2006: Figure 1).

the base of the pyramid, on the north-south axis (called "Burial 2"). Placed in the chamber was a complete adult male skeleton, aged 40–50. His hands were crossed behind his back as if they had been tied. The chamber also contained animal remains and greenstone figurines, and the remains of another person was represented by the back part of the skull, which exhibited scraping and cut-marks (Spence and Pereira 2007: 147–148).

At the construction of Building 5, around 300 CE, two deposits were found. Burial 3 was on the north-south axis at the base of the pyramid, and Burial 6 in the centre of the building. Burial 3 contained four complete human skeletons and animal skulls. The humans were centrally placed, three in an extended position, and the fourth slightly apart from the others in a very flexed position. They all had their arms crossed behind their back, and their lower legs were very close, as if these may also have been bound. The extended individuals were all male, aged 18–20, 20–24, and 40–44. Sex could not be assigned to the last, younger individual aged 13–15 (Spence and Pereira 2007: 149). Burial 6 contained 12 individuals, all appearing to have had their hands bound behind their back. Skeletons 6A and 6B were complete, wore fine regalia, were spatially separate from the others, and one had been treated with red pigment, while the other displayed dental modification. The rest had no finery, were piled together, and had all been decapitated. All identifiable individuals were males aged 18–44 (Spence and Pereira 2007: 152–153; Pereira and Chávez 2006).

The construction of Building 6 also had two deposits associated with it – Burial 4 and Burial 5, dated to around 350 CE. Burial 4 was once again placed at the base of the pyramid on the north-south axis. In it were the heads of 17 individuals, and an 18th was represented by a vertebra. The heads had been deposited prior to the decomposition of the flesh, and at least one vertebra, and in many cases more, were still present. Some displayed cutmarks and signs of decapitation, and red pigment were found on all but one. All but one showed signs of cranial deformation and at least 10 individuals had dental modifications in the form of inlays of pyrite, jadeite, and greenstone.[46] All identifiable remains

---

[46] Cranial and dental modifications may both signal a specific status, and the type could be a geographical indicator. A preoccupation with teeth can also de identified in the

were from males, aged 18–50; two could not be assigned sex, but were aged 14–15 and 18 (Spence and Pereira 2007: 149–151). Burial 5 was on the midline of the upper platform (rather than at the base as the other deposits), and held three complete human skeletons, accompanied by animal skeletons of pumas, rattlesnakes, and an eagle. The bodies had been placed in a seated position, with hands in front of them, possibly bound, but this is more difficult to determine here. All the bodies had been deposited simultaneously, and had been left in the open to decompose. Skeletons 5A and 5B had been treated with red pigment while in the seated position; 5 C had not and also seemed placed slightly apart. All were male, ranging in age between 40–70 (Spence and Pereira 2007: 151–152).

The Feathered Serpent Pyramid, also called Temple of Quetzalcoatl, is the main feature of the Ciudadela complex, or Citadel, east of the Avenue of the Dead and south of the Sun and Moon Pyramids. It was constructed around 200 CE. In the foundations and construction of the pyramid over 137 burials of men and women[47] had been placed, most, if not all, sacrificial victims. The graves were both multiple and single, and symbolic personal offerings identifying their role were carefully placed with most of the bodies.

Saburo Sugiyama has carried out an extensive study of distributional patterns based on factors such as placement, gender, body position and direction, skeleton cluster numbers, and associated finds (Sugiyama 2005). The results are fascinating, and demonstrate very clear patterns: the bodies are placed in symbolically significant locations that reflect not only the building's design (for example, a burial in each corner of the pyramid), but

elaborate 'maxilla necklaces' made of real human and animal teeth, and shell imitation, found in the Feathered Serpent Pyramid and elsewhere (Sugiyama 2005: 171–179).

[47] The structure has not been fully excavated – Sugiyama estimates a total of over 200 individuals (Sugiyama 2005: 7).

possibly also larger astronomical and calendrical concerns, with time being expressed in spatial terms (Sugiyama 2005: 50–52, 220–223). Similar concerns may be reflected in the number of people in each deposit, which, along with other military iconography and finds, point to a relation to warfare, sacrifice, water/the underworld, and authority or transfer or authority. The central Grave 14 contained 20 male soldiers with their equipment – the Mayan word for war and warrior is the same as that for 20, and this also seems relevant for the Teotihuacanos. Other graves contain reference to the numbers 1, 4, 8, 9, and 20, which appear to form sub-sets that relate to the 260-day calendar (Sugiyama 2005: 90, 97–98). In general, the bodies were also placed with the heads towards the centre of the pyramid, as can especially be seen in the graves in the southern and eastern areas; if the facial direction is instead taken into account, the direction is outward, away from the pyramid, "as if guarding it" (Sugiyama 2005: 104–105, Figure 41, and 105). Cause of death has in most cases not been determined, but many of the bodies seem to have had their hands bound behind them, and if possible cases of binding in front are added, this accounts for 91 per cent of the individuals (Sugiyama 2005: 109). The single skeleton from Grave 15 shows indications of heart excision (Sugiyama 2005: 26, 89).[48]

The creation of extremely symbolically charged spaces is evident in both the Pyramid of the Moon and the Feathered Serpent Pyramid. In both cases, everything is very carefully laid out, and no element is random or accidental. The placement of all deposits, in transitional spaces (both geographically and chronologically, between physical structures and between the building of them

---

[48] This grave may in fact predate the structure itself (Sugiyama 2005: 88–89), meaning that it would not have been part of the event that resulted in the remaining burials, but if it does contain a victim of sacrifice, it testifies to the longevity of the sacred space.

in time), reveals their significance as related to the construction of new buildings – even (or perhaps especially) if these are built on top of previous remains.[49] It is also clear that the appropriate sacrificial victims were in large part young to middle-aged men for the rituals at the Moon Pyramid, while both men and women were sacrificed at the Feathered Serpent Pyramid. In the latter, the men are fitted out as warriors, and clear differentiation is made between men and women based on their associated finds (each grave also appears to have had only men or only women, and the female graves were mostly in peripheral areas). One very interesting exception is one of the males in Burial 14 (14-M), where some sort of gender blurring or reversal appears to have taken place (Sugiyama 2005: 180).[50]

Many of the individuals in both places were either in fact high-ranking individuals or manipulated to appear as such. The offerings or finds (sometimes lack thereof) are not personal items reflecting personal identity, but rather carefully set up to represent whatever 'character' or player is considered appropriate for each particular ritual – in these cases, especially male warriors. The construction of new buildings may in turn, as convincingly argued by Sugiyama for the Feathered Serpent Pyramid (Sugiyama 2005: 231–236), be related to the accession of a new ruler. Accession and sacrifice, autosacrifice, or bloodletting have been shown to be closely connected in Maya iconography (Schele and Miller 1992), with both men and women performing the act – women for example by piercing their tongue and passing rope or cloth through to shed more blood, men by piercing their penis. At Tenochtitlan, a room in the

---

[49] Welsh lists Classic period examples of 'caches' in stone boxes or ceramic containers with possible remains of human sacrifices, placed under stelae, altars, temple stairs, and structural foundations (Welsh 1988: 170, 181–183, table 103).

[50] This biologically male individual was not associated with items only worn by men in the FSP, but instead with those usually associated with women.

House of Eagles has been identified that was probably designated specifically for the purpose of bloodletting, as copious amounts of human blood were found on the floor (López Luján and Levin 2006: 32). It seems likely that in these cases, the new building activities took place in connection with the accession of a new ruler, and sacrifice was intimately linked with the associated ceremonies and ideology, as well as the perceived structural integrity of the buildings.[51]

Skull Racks and Ball Games

Ball courts are common Terminal Classic and Postclassic structures found especially at Maya and Aztec sites, but also elsewhere. The ball game may go as far back as Olmec times in some areas (Wilkerson 1984: 116), and certainly Early Classic courts are known from several sites (Miller 1999: 357).[52] They are typically described and depicted as I-shaped, with two long, parallel structures with either vertical or sloping sides. The game is played between these. At either end, there may be related buildings such as temples. The exact nature of the game is disputed, but it seems that the players on two teams would manipulate a rubber ball by bouncing it off their hips, knees, and elbows. One way of 'scoring' was probably by passing the ball through the rings usually found on the sides of the court, although the difficulty of this makes it likely that this was not the only way of winning points. The fact that ball courts vary in size and details of features (even within the same site) suggests that there were several versions of the game. In at least one version, there is strong evidence that the losing party was sacrificed, and in this case, the game itself may

---

[51] Evidence of sacrifice associated with construction was also found at Chalchuapa in El Salvador (Fowler 1984) and at El Coyote in Honduras (Berryman 2007: 393).

[52] Discussions and surveys of known ball courts can be found in the papers in Scarborough and Wilcox 1993.

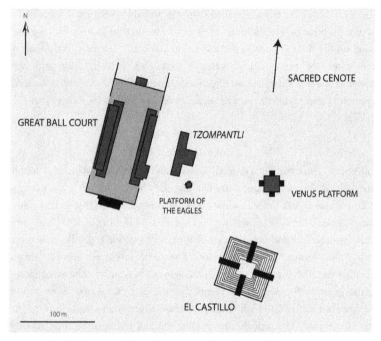

Figure 30 Chichen Itza, plan of area near the Great Ball Court.

represent a ritual, controlled re-enactment of warfare (Schele and Miller 1992: 249–252).

The most famous court, the Great Ball Court at Chichen Itza (Figures 30 and 31), has elaborate reliefs on both sides, depicting a ball player who has just been decapitated (Figure 32), and seven snakes sprouting out of his neck. The sacrificer seems to be the winning player, who holds his opponent's head with blood flowing out of it in one hand, and his instrument of sacrifice,

Figure 31 Chichen Itza Great Ball Court, view from the south (photo by Emma Saunders).

presumably an obsidian blade, in the other. Other examples from Chichen Itza are found in the Red House ball court (Structure 3C10) and ball court 3D4 (Ruppert 1952: Figures 124b-c and 129 c-d).

The same association can be found on a Late Classic stele from Aparicio, Veracruz, where seven snakes protrude from the neck of a decapitated ball player, recognisable by his kneepad, waist protector, *palma*,[53] and

[53] *Palmas* are a kind of trophy carried by ball players; one can be seen to the right of the player on the Aparicio stele. Actual examples have been found in excavations, and

Figure 32 Chichen Itza Great Ball Court relief (redrawn after Schele and Miller 1992: Figure VI.3).

hammerstone or stone weight (Moser 1973: 17, Figure 13). The South Ball Court at El Tajin has panels showing rituals related to the game in a cartoon-like sequence (Epiclassic, Wilkerson 1984: 119–125; Coe and Koontz 2013: 146–149). The first three panels depict preparatory rituals and a moment just before the game itself; the fourth panel shows the losing player being decapitated (or stabbed?) with a flint knife by another player and held back by a third (Figure 33). Wilkerson suggests that all the actors on the panel in fact impersonate gods, supporting the idea of a ritual/mythical battle (Wilkerson 1984: 123).

In iconography related to the ball game, the ball itself is often conflated with a human head – in the Chichen Itza relief, the ball with a human skull

one from Coatepec, Veracruz depicts a player holding up a severed human head (Moser 1973: Figure 14). A link with heart excision can be seen on another *palma* where the player has had his heart removed (depicted in Miller 2001: Figure 75).

Figure 33 El Tajin South Ball Court panel (redrawn after Wilkerson 1984: Figure 14).

inside appears between the two players.[54] At Coba, in the Late Classic Group D ball court, two 'markers' in the form of a round relief with a decapitated jaguar and a stone human skull had been placed in the floor of the court.

---

[54] The ball court associated with the so-called Church at Chichen Itza has a similar motif on the reliefs (Bolles 1977: 226). Another version is the whole human body bound up as a ball, e.g., Schele and Miller 1992: 251, Figure VI.8–9.

Whether or not this means that actual human heads were used in the game cannot be proven, but there is a clear focus on and fascination with human heads and skulls. This is supported by another common Classic/Postclassic type of structure, usually called a skull rack or *tzompantli*.[55] These are usually found in association with ball courts or temples, which is undoubtedly not accidental. At Chichen Itza, a *tzompantli* is located immediately east of the Great Ball Court. On the sides of the structure, over 2400 human skulls are carved in relief, placed on vertical poles (Figure 34). Only two actual human skulls had been placed within the *tzompantli* at Chichen Itza, but along the important *sacbe 1*[56] many human remains, especially parts of the skull, were recovered, and it has been suggested that these were also placed on poles and displayed along the road (Miller 2007: 170–171). At the Aztec site of Tlatelolco (c. 1337–1521 CE), on the other hand, 170 human skulls were found arranged in neat groups near the Great Pyramid. The skulls had signs of decapitation, skinning and defleshing, and large holes in the sides, in this case to be strung on horizontal poles (Pijoan Aguadé and Lory 1997: 236). The 100 skulls studied by Pijoan Aguadé and Lory had an almost equal distribution between men and women, aged 18–40 (1997: 222).

The ball game could have a strong symbolic element, re-enacting battles by forcing defeated captives to take part (in iconography, high ranking individuals are sometimes identified with a name glyph on their femur – Schele and Miller 1992: 249), and/or re-enacting the myth of the Hero Twins Hunahpu and Xbalanque, who went to the underworld and played the game

---

[55] Miller (1999) and Mendoza (2007b) offer discussions and overviews of *tzompantlis*, including early wooden examples and the association of the ball game and decapitation, and extensive references to further studies on the topic.

[56] A *sacbe* (plural *sacbeoob*) is a raised, artificial road, especially typical of the Yucatan area, some going as far as 100 km (Morley and Brainerd 1983: 333–335).

Figure 34 Chichen Itza *tzompantli* (photo by Emma Saunders).

with the underworld gods.[57] Each day, they were forced to play again and had to outwit the gods in order to survive. Decapitation and play with the head feature in the myth. The ball court and *tzompantli* were thus connected to the

---

[57] As recorded in the *Popol Vuh*, a sixteenth century Quiche Maya document. This document itself was perhaps conceived as a performance (Schele and Miller 1992: 32).

underworld, and the court itself may have been perceived as a portal or cleft to it, as suggested by Mendoza (2007b: 410, 418).

Skulls are also found in temples in what appear to be non-funerary contexts. A Postclassic temple at Ixlú in northern Guatemala (Structure 2023) was found to contain neatly arranged skulls in the building platform and altar (Duncan 2011). Two skulls were in the altar, two just in front, two just west of the structure, 15 in two rows in the platform, and dismembered postcranial remains of four individuals were found on the east side (Figure 35) (Duncan 2011: 555). The postcranial remains were all of males aged 15–35; the skulls could not be determined with certainty, but some were probably male, and all young to middle adults. In addition, at least three of the individuals were related, giving some clue to the make-up of the victims. Vertebrae in articulation suggest decapitation, and Duncan interprets the context as construction sacrifice since the skulls were deposited prior to building (Duncan 2011: 565), in line with those discussed earlier.[58]

Removal of the Heart

Returning for a moment to Chichen Itza and the relation between ball court and *tzompantli*, we can in the same place find an association between these and another common theme in human sacrifice: that of removal or excision of the heart. Most likely this was done while the victim was still alive. Eagles and jaguars are shown eating human hearts both on the *tzompantli* itself and on the adjacent Platform of the Eagles and the Jaguars (Figure 36). Based on an anatomical-surgical approach, Robicsek and Hales thought the most likely technique for removing the heart was a bilateral transverse thoracotomy (1984:

---

[58] A good survey of further evidence of decapitation in iconography and archaeological contexts, including very early ones, can be found in Moser (1973). Duncan (2011) offers additional archaeological examples from nonfunerary Postclassic contexts.

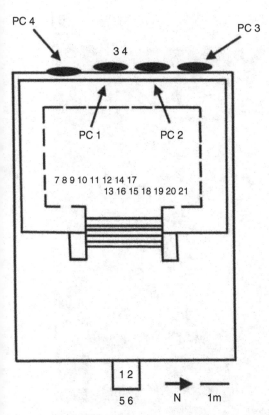

Figure 35 Ixlú Structure 2023 Temple with location of skeletal remains (after Duncan 2011: Figure 3. Courtesy of William N. Duncan).

Figure 36 Chichen Itza *tzompantli*, eagle eating human heart (photo by Emma Saunders).

82–84), where a cut is made over the ribs across the entire torso (rather than just the side of the heart) to provide the best access to the heart. Most recently, Tiesler and Cucina have argued a slightly different approach, where the heart is accessed by cutting just below and beneath the ribs, which should also be a faster method (2006: 504, 506).

Depictions of heart removal show the human body extended on its back over a large stone or altar; the extension is sometimes helped by somebody holding legs and/or arms outstretched. The torso is then cut open with a blade, and the heart removed. One particularly relevant example comes from the Temple of the Jaguars, which is in fact part of the Great Ball Court at Chichen Itza (Morley and Brainerd 1983: 463, Figure14.1e). Two other examples from Chichen Itza are found in the Temple of the Warriors and depicted on a gold disc from the Cenote of Sacrifice (or sacred well – Figure 37).[59] On these, we can clearly see how the body is extended and flexed in order to facilitate the excision. The act requires skill, and the sacrificer himself was most likely an expert; he wears elaborate warrior-like regalia different from the other characters in the scenes. Each performer seems to have had a very specific role to play in the ritual, as their stances and clothes suggest. On the gold disc, we see on the right another person wearing a cape and feather-capped headdress bringing in the next victim, who is instead nearly naked and with the long hair signifying a captive (Schele and Miller 1992: 54).

Post-excision images also occur, where the heart has been removed and the chest is shown open. In stelae from Piedras Negras, something

---

[59] The cenote also contained remains of human sacrificial victims thrown into the well, dated to the Postclassic period, but cannot be assigned with certainty to either of its two phases (Coggins and Shane 1984: 26). Various records of the human bones suggest that children and subadults are particularly prevalent, with a marginal preference for males in the adults (Ediger 1971: 141; Beck and Sievert 2005; Tiesler 2007).

Figure 37 Chichen Itza Cenote, gold disc (redrawn after Miller 2001: Figure 2).

emerges from the open chest (Figure 38) – perhaps a graphic of the association between sacrifice and regeneration or fertility (maize is associated with blood and even cannibalism in Aztec mythology, where human sacrifice is needed to restore the god Centeotl, who is symbolically eaten

Figure 38 Piedra Negras stele 11, post-excision (redrawn after Schele and Miller 1992: Figure II.4).

when humans eat maize). Sometimes several types of mutilation are shown simultaneously, as in a scene from a column at El Tajin, where heart excision or disembowelment appear to take place simultaneously (Figure 39).

Figure 39 El Tajin column showing decapitation and disembowelment (redrawn after Wilkerson 1984: Figure 10).

Heart sacrifice is not often identified (or indeed identifiable) in the osteological and archaeological records. Good examples have been analysed by Tiesler and Cucina (2006). One example comes from Calakmul Tomb 4, in Structure II, thought to belong to one of the site's rulers (Yuknom Yich'ak K'ak) and dated to c. 700 CE (Carrasco Vargas et al. 1999 for report on the main burial). The main occupant was placed in a vaulted chamber, while two 'attendants' were found in a small antechamber: a woman in her thirties and a 10–12 year old child, probably male. They had been deposited simultaneously, likely just after the sealing of the main chamber. The women had chop marks on the twelfth interior thoracic vertebra (Tiesler and Cucina 2006: 498).

Another sacrifice carried out in connection with the construction of a building can be found at Classic period Becán, where the skeleton of a 15–18 year old individual (possibly male) was found at the bottom of a sealed staircase of Complex X (Tiesler and Campaña Valenzuela 2003). Marks were found on the 12th thoracic vertebra, similar to those from Calakmul (Tiesler and Cucina 2006: 500). These marks in turn mirror those found on one of the five-six 'attendant' individuals in a box outside the Tomb of Janaab' Pakal in the Temple of Inscriptions at Palenque (Classic period, Tiesler and Cucina 2006: 502–503; Cucina and Tiesler 2006: 106–112).

After the sacrifice, the heart may have been placed in the small receptacle of a so-called *chacmool*. A *chacmool* is a reclining human stone sculpture facing upwards and holding a bowl or similar in its hands (Figure 40), often associated with sacred structures. They are believed to have the function of holding the excised heart in sacrifice.[60] Although this is largely speculation, the presence of one such sculpture in the Tenochtitlan Templo Mayor may support this interpretation. The Templo Mayor had double shrines on the top – one dedicated to Tlaloc, the god of rain, life, and growth, the other to Huitzilopochtli, the god of war and the sun. In front of the Huitzilopochtli shrine was a stone altar; in the same location in front of the Tlaloc was instead a *chacmool* (Matos 1988: 66). At Chichen Itza, three *chacmools* were associated with the *tzompantli*, including two found inside the structure (Ruppert 1952:

---

[60] The exact origin and meaning of *chacmools* are a matter of debate. Miller (1985) believes them to ultimately be of Maya origin and represent defeated captives. Carlson feels they fit Toltec iconography better, and suggests an appealing interpretation of them as ball players in a characteristic in-game position (Carlson 2013).

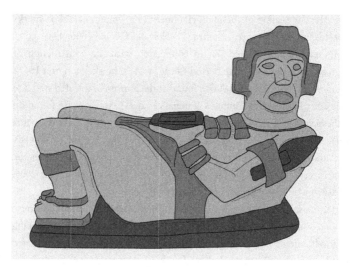

Figure 40 *Chacmool* from Tula, height 66 cm (drawn after Diehl 1983: pl. XII).

166), and a famous *chacmool* from Tula has a sacrificial knife strapped to its arm (Diehl 1983: pl. XII).

Retainer and Mortuary Sacrifice

Mesoamerican cultures join in the practice of retainer and other mortuary sacrifice. Other elaborate mortuary and ancestor veneration activities include wrapping and bundling of remains, painting or sprinkling of bones with cinnabar or hematite, successive multiple burials, later re-entry of tomb, disturbance, removal and movement of parts of skeletons, and in rare cases, possibly cutting or other types of processing of bones (see, e.g., Fitzsimmons 2009 for elaborate discussion of some these). These can be difficult to distinguish from sacrificial activities, and indeed in some cases it may not make sense to do so – for example, later, commemorative events may involve animal and human sacrifices. Nevertheless, useful guiding criteria for identifying sacrificial versus funerary practices in the Mesoamerican sphere[61] have been offered by Tiesler (2007: 22–23) and Berryman (2007: 394), where the focus is on treatment and position of remains compared to funerary ones, presence and types of offerings, and osteological evidence of cause of death and postsacrificial activities.

The practice goes back at least to the Preclassic period, with possible cases from Los Mangales, Guatemala (Sharer and Sedat 1987: 136–138) and Sin Cabeza, Guatemala (Berryman 2007: 390).

At Classic period Palenque, we saw (above) that the ruler Janaab' Pakal was accompanied by five-six 'attendants'. In this case, Cucina and Tiesler interpret the context as coming from a later commemoration event honouring the deceased and taking place perhaps months after the main interment (2006: 123–124).[62] From Palenque, there is another burial with companion sacrifices: a sarcophagus containing an elderly female was found in a temple (called "Reina Roja", or the "Red Queen"), from the Classic period. She was accompanied by a female 'attendant' aged about 30 on one side of the tomb, and an 8–10 year old on the other side. The attendants were both face down and the woman had her arms crossed behind her back. Cut and stab marks were found on ribs and vertebrae of the woman, suggesting several severe blows from

---

[61] These cannot blindly be adapted for other areas, as they depend on the social, religious, and political practices of the region; however, they might serve as a useful base to develop similar criteria elsewhere.

[62] An alternative explanation is suggested by Weiss-Krejci (2003) for this and other burials with sacrificial victims. Her caution in not simply assuming every simultaneous burial is a sacrifice is warranted, but the evidence presented by Cucina and Tiesler provides a persuasive case for sacrifice.

behind or the side, possibly cutting the body in two.[63] The child had cutmarks on the third cervical vertebra, achieved by a severe blow from behind to a forward-flexed neck – probably a decapitation (Tiesler and Cucina 2006: 502; Cucina and Tiesler 2006: 112–117). Additional possible examples of retainer and mortuary sacrifices have been suggested for Santa Luisa (El Tajin region, Classic/Epiclassic, Wilkerson 1984: 108), Piedras Negras (Coe 1959: 131), and Tikal Burial 10 (Wright 2005).[64]

Discussion

The evidence from Mesoamerica offers the greatest variety of means of sacrifice, sacrificial participants, and the contexts in which it could take place, both in terms of archaeology and iconography. It is also where some of the best and most promising osteological studies have been undertaken, and future research has the potential to reveal further details of practices related to human bones. The victim could be killed by decapitation, throat slashing, heart excision, spears, or arrows (or a combination of these), and subsequently might be flayed, defleshed, dismembered, ritually consumed, and/or reanimated.[65] Most of these are recorded in iconography, on skeletal remains and in the colonial sources.

---

[63] Victims are shown cut in two on a Protoclassic stele in the Hauberg Collection (Schele and Miller 1992: 191, pl. 66b).

[64] Welsh also provides an extensive list of possible companion sacrifices at Classic Lowland Maya sites (Welsh 1988: 176–181, 184–185, tables 101, 102, 104). Although Welsh considers all of them sacrifices, other interpretations may be relevant in some cases (McAnany 1995: 62–32).

[65] For example, flaying and dismemberment in the art from Cotzumalguapa, Guatemala (Chinchilla Mazariegos 2014); scalping as part of closure ritual deposit at Baking Pot, Belize (Piehl and Awe 2010); possible cannibalism, see Pijoan Aguadé and Lory

The victims often appear to have been war captives (warfare was even in some cases specifically carried out in order to obtain people for sacrifice); they could also be high ranking individuals, and there is some suggestions that the higher the rank, the more prestigious the victim. Others were certainly also sacrificed, but we know less about them. What we do know is that men, women, and children of all ages could be sacrificed, but certain types of individuals may have been considered more suitable for specific sacrifices. It also seems that although all categories were possible, in many sacrifices, young men of fighting age were preferred, as can be seen in relation to new construction phases at Teotihuacan.

The sacrifices could be major public events with a high level of visibility, as seems especially evident in later periods. In other cases, they are more subtle, focussing on fewer victims and being only one part of much more extended rituals. Elite displays and use of human sacrifice had strong associations with negotiations of power and authority, based on beliefs that appear to reflect cosmological concerns. The manipulation of human bones in many different settings blurs the boundaries between sacrifice, ancestor worship, mortuary practices, and secular violence (see, e.g., Harrison-Buck et al. 2007). Skeletons are taken apart, bones painted and re-used, often incorporated and made part of structures. This happens in the building sacrifices considered above, but also in intriguing arrangements, where for example human femurs were found imbedded in the walls of the inner Castillo at Chichen Itza (Miller 2007). Skulls are part of this practice in an almost obsessive fashion, as exemplified by the elaborate displays on skull racks and ball courts, and in caches associated with buildings and travel paths. They were certainly meant to be seen by both humans and non-humans.

(1997). Reanimation can occur in the use of human faces as masks (see, e.g., Harrison-Buck et al. 2007: Figure 4.7; Matos Moctezuma 1988: Figures 79 and 80).

7 Conclusion

From the riches of Ur through the muddy naked bodies of Denmark and Ireland to the intricate, dental-embellished warriors of Teotihuacan, human sacrifice offers its own story of how we express identity and engage with supernatural entities. There is plenty to think about, including images of heart removal, evidence of decapitation, and direct face-to-face encounters with people of the past.

With the possible exceptions of certain Mesoamerican groups and the relatively short period of Shang occupation at Anyang, human sacrifice is not an integral part of any one group's rituals and social activity. Human sacrifice is otherwise quite rare. Conceptually, it does not differ significantly from animal sacrifice, other than humans possibly being perceived as of higher value. Human victims are repeatedly found within the same system as animals (and other offerings). This is clear in every geographical area discussed here: just a few examples include donkeys at the funerary enclosures of Abydos, cattle in the tombs of Ur, equids at Tell Umm el-Marra, horses, elephants, and dogs at Xibeigang, horses in the bogs of Denmark, and pumas and rattlesnakes at Teotihuacan. We may then assume that the occasions and reasons for human sacrifice were not so very different from those of other animals, perhaps only with a stronger incentive or need for symbolic elements.

Generally speaking, there seems to be no biological or social limits to the kinds of human considered appropriate for sacrifice. We have encountered women, men (possibly even gender blurring), and children, from infancy to adulthood. Individuals of unusual physical stature or with physical abnormalities appear, and these are only the ones we can identify from bones alone. This also says nothing about possible mental status, which we are unfortunately not able to determine, but which may well have played an important role in some instances. We have also seen that the (actual or created) social status of the victim can vary greatly, from likely slaves and war captives through warriors/ soldiers and court attendants to the closest family members of rulers.

This overall lack of preference does not mean that anything goes at any time, anywhere. In many cases, we can be certain that the victims were very carefully chosen so as to produce a meaningful complete assemblage. This applies to most examples of retainer sacrifice, as well as careful arrangements like those at the Feathered Serpent Pyramid at Teotihuacan and the funerary enclosures at Abydos. In other cases, only certain victims were used, whether by requirement or availability. And although a varied demographic is represented, not all are equally common. Men of fighting age appear to be particularly popular, as seen in much of the Mesoamerican and Shang material. These are also the cases with the strongest evidence for captives as victims and for a more pervasive role of sacrifice, where actions specifically aimed at acquiring victims for rituals may have been necessary. As such, sacrifice and violence may feed each other.

We know much more about the victims than those sacrificing, since the sacrificers are only indirectly present. There are no specifics about the person holding the knife, so to speak. However, since in most cases, a central liturgy was in place, and sacrifice would have been part of this and likely also require a practical skill set, we can assume that the sacrificer was part of this. Specialised personnel such as priests are the most obvious,[66] but there may also have been those specifically trained in certain types of killing, as has been suggested for the Maya (Robicsek and Hales 1984: 59–60). The entire ritual, however, was sanctioned (and often commissioned) by rulers, whether local

---

[66] For the period of the Spanish arrival in Mesoamerica, priests are most vividly and repeatedly described in the writings of Bernal Díaz as covered in blood and performing sacrifices wherever they went (see his *The true history of the conquest of New Spain*).

or of larger territories. Discrete levels of functions and reasons for sacrifice may be represented by individual actors (the priest may act out of mostly personal beliefs, while the ruler may have an added political agenda).

Sacrifice as Theatre and Memory

The diversity of human sacrifice as discussed here can hardly be over-emphasised. However, there are a few 'types', which seem to occur in several places with shared features.

The most common type of sacrifice is that of mortuary and retainer sacrifices. Found in Mesoamerica, China, Egypt, and the Near East, it is characterised by relatively large numbers of victims, an incredible wealth of goods, and larger sized tombs. The entire assemblages are such that they would provide an impressive display of power, ideal for processions and ritual enactments at or near the tomb. Generally speaking, retainer sacrifice appears to be an elite, if not entirely royal prerogative. It is revealing that this type of sacrifice is nearly always associated with a royal person, most often a king (though sometimes also queens). The analogy of a play does seem most apt (used by e.g., Dickson 2006), albeit with a much too real ending. Identities may be simulated or real, although especially the material from Egypt suggests that real identities are reflected by the finds. Whether real or simulated, they are at their most intense, like a modern-day bride and groom in their very finest attire. But if the entire event is a play and the human and animal retainers the actors and whichever elements of the population are allowed to watch is the audience, who is the director? This is perhaps a crucial clue to understanding the shared features in this ritual across cultures. The deceased king or queen would likely have prepared provisions and building of the tomb, but when the time comes, the play itself must necessarily be directed by someone else. This someone else is most likely the next in line. In Mesoamerica, we have seen the close connection between sacrifice, kingship, and accession (and here, the idea of ritual re-enactment becomes particularly apt in connection with the ball "games"). Although less explicit, it seems that a similar association occurred in Egypt, China, and the Near East. If the identification of the tombs as royal holds true, retainer sacrifice happened precisely when the throne shifted from one individual to another, and thus seems to be part of an agenda to legitimise the new king or queen. That is as far as the play goes for the living.

The possible ideological and political agendas of mortuary sacrifices are built on religious beliefs and practices, otherwise they would be inefficient. In mortuary sacrifices, we may distinguish between those related to funerary rituals, and those associated with later rituals, possibly as part of ancestor worship/vocation or commemorative rites. Sacrifices taking place at a funeral could be either directly related to the main deceased, or to other supernatural entities. Individuals found in close proximity to the deceased and with a diverse demographic are most likely also directly related to him/her. This is often clear in the spatial distribution of victims, as at Anyang, where those placed in the same chamber as the deceased appear to be family members, while those in passages, *yaokeng*, and small tombs separate from the main tomb serve a different, more symbolic function. Individuals placed in separate spaces that are not clearly linked to the event of the funeral may be those related to ancestor worship and commemorative rituals. An example of this is the small Xibeigang tombs, where the bone inscriptions help significantly by telling us that sacrifice was in particular a way of communicating with ancestors.

Human remains are also frequently found within or closely associated with architectural elements. We find examples of this in the early period of Mesopotamian history, in some of the sacred spaces at Anyang, and in structures in Mesoamerica, e.g., at Teotihuacan, Chichen Itza, and Ixlú. Although different in their details, an element of memory or commemoration appears to be part of these. At Teotihuacan, the sacrifices are very directly related to structural additions, while at Nuzi and Tepe Gawra, they are incorporated into walls and floors. The sacrifices are embedded into the 'skeleton' of structures, becoming *part of* buildings. As such, they continue to exist for as long as the building exists, and may be remembered for the same length of time. The purpose of this embedding may range from a desire to sanctify a space, through perceived protective abilities, to the need to 'feed' a building, or the creation of a symbolic cosmic arrangement. It is not always possible to determine which of these (or other) interpretations fit the best (and several may be at play simultaneously), but the types of victims can be a clue (individuals dressed as warriors or soldiers seem more likely candidates for a protective purpose than infants, for example), as can the type of building and position and arrangement of victims.

Liminality and the Power of the Hidden

The high visibility suggested by mortuary sacrifices is often coupled with a hidden element, or at least one hidden from human eyes. Sacrificial remains as we find them are nearly always deliberately removed from view by being placed in the ground or inside structural elements. The most fascinating of these are when the human remains and other offerings are nevertheless meticulously and symbolically arranged: clearly for *someone* or *something* to see and appreciate, but not humans. Returning to the tombs at Ur, the sheer amount of wealth, detail in individual outfits, and arrangement of victims in PG 789, PG 800, and PG 1237 reveal a deliberate and carefully thought-out display. This is even more striking at the Teotihuacan Feathered Serpent Pyramid, where the arrangement is a much more complex web of symmetrical and symbolic relations between the victims, the building, the site, and cosmological space. A more modest example is the Tell Umm el-Marra Tomb 1, where symmetrical relations and careful positioning of bodies and finds can also be found. In all these cases, the complete assemblage has been covered and removed from circulation. A large amount of labour (skilled and unskilled, directly and indirectly) and economic wealth have gone into these assemblages, yet been removed from all practical uses. This testifies to their significance, even though invisible to the human eye. Or more likely, precisely because they are not visible. The invisible has a certain unexplained power in human terms (some of the horror films considered the scariest are those where the 'evil' remains unseen; the power of the imagination is often much greater than reality). More importantly, the sacrifices and all that goes with them are visible and accessible to supernatural beings. Their placement away from human view and *within* sacred space is thus clearly designated for appreciation by deities, spirits, ancestors, and other supernatural beings.

A further indication of this is the physical placement of victims. In all types of sacrifice, they are often placed in liminal spaces. Liminal spaces are those *between* worlds, where normal conditions may be reversed or blurred and contact between spheres become possible. They are thus particularly suited for ritual purposes. Physically, such spaces can be thresholds, walls, corners, floors, dromoi/passages in tombs, and spaces directly in front of or surrounding structures. We frequently see human remains located in precisely these places, and whether or not they always represent sacrifices, they can serve the purpose of blending and creating connections between worlds. Liminal spaces can also be broader environments believed to embody mystical features. The bogs of northern Europe are good examples of this kind of space, being between land and sea, swallowing up things that come near them and often covered by mist. The bodies placed here are also quickly hidden, yet preserved, providing a different version of the importance of both that which is hidden yet embedded (and remembered?).

Human Sacrifice and Archaeology

The archaeology of human sacrifice is as enigmatic and challenging as ever. It may raise more questions than it answers, but it does not leave us entirely clueless. It offers serious engagement with past ritual activities and a glimpse of the negotiations between identity, religious beliefs, and sacred space, political power, and memory. Recent approaches to the study of human bones and distribution within archaeological contexts illustrate how we may continue to learn more about the practice, along with new possible discoveries in future excavations. Regardless, the extreme nature of human sacrifice will continue to be a highly relevant topic and provide clues to understanding the extreme actions carried out by humans throughout history.

Appendix

Possible Cases of Human Sacrifice from Other Periods and Areas around the World

As space does not permit a comprehensive discussion of all possible cases of human sacrifice in archaeological contexts from around the world, this appendix provides bibliographical references for further study. The references offered are envisioned as introductory, many providing case studies and/or further avenues for in-depth study.

Europe

Good overall discussion with many examples especially from northern, western and central Europe:

Aldhouse-Green, Miranda. 2001. *Dying for the Gods: Human Sacrifice in Iron Age and Roman Europe*. Stroud: Tempus.

Ritual deposits of skulls in Germany:

Orschiedt, Jörg. 2015. "Die Große Ofnet-Höhle: Ein steinzeitliches Massakre?" In *Krieg – eine archäologische Spurensuche*, edited by Harald Meller, Michael Schefzik, and Peter Ettel, 99–102. Darmstadt: Theiss, Konrad.

Ritualised cannibalism with possible sacrifice, Germany:

Boulestin, Bruno, Andrea Zeeb-Lanz, Christian Jeunesse, Fabian Haack, Rose-Marie Arbogast, and Anthony Denaire. 2009. "Mass Cannibalism in the

Linear Pottery Culture at Herxheim (Palatinate, Germany)." *Antiquity* 83 (322): 968–982.

Bronze Age Greece:

Hughes, Dennis D. 1991. *Human Sacrifice in Ancient Greece*. London: Routledge.

Sakellarakis, Yannis, and Efi Sapouna-Sakellaraki. 1991. *Archanes*. Athens: Ekdotike Athenon.

Viking sacrificial well deposits:

Gotfredsen, Anne Birgitte, Charlotte Primeau, Karin Margarita Frei, and Lars Jørgensen. 2014. "A Ritual Site with Sacrificial Wells from the Viking Age at Trelleborg, Denmark." *Danish Journal of Archaeology* 3 (2): 145–63.

South America

Peruvian human sacrifice (especially Inca and Moche):

Benson, Elizabeth P., and Anita G. Cook, eds. 2001. *Ritual Sacrifice in Ancient Peru*. Austin: University of Texas Press.

Bourget, Steve. 2006. *Sex, Death, and Sacrifice in Moche Religion and Visual Culture*. Austin: University of Texas Press.

Eeckhout, Peter, and Lawrence Stewart Owens. 2008. "Human Sacrifice at Pachacamac." *Latin American Antiquity* 19 (4): 375–98.

Toyne, J. Maria, Christine D. White, John W. Verano, Santiago Uceda Castillo, Jean François Millaire, and Fred J. Longstaffe. 2014. "Residential Histories of Elites and Sacrificial Victims at Huacas de Moche, Peru, as Reconstructed from Oxygen Isotopes." *Journal of Archaeological Science* 42: 15–28.

Verano, John W. 2005. "Human Sacrifice and Postmortem Modification at the Pyramid of the Moon, Moche Valley, Peru." In *Interacting with the Dead: Perspectives on Mortuary Archaeology for the New Millennium*, edited by Gordon F.M. Rakita, Jane E. Buikstra, Lane A. Beck, and Sloan R. Williams, 277–89. Gainesville: University Press of Florida.

North America

Cahokia Mound 72:

Young, Biloine W., and Melvin Leo Fowler. 2000. *Cahokia, the Great Native American Metropolis*. Urbana and Chicago: University of Illinois Press.

Africa

Nubia mortuary sacrifice:

Buzon, Michele R., and Margaret A. Judd. 2008. "Investigating Health at Kerma: Sacrificial versus Nonsacrificial Individuals." *American Journal of Physical Anthropology* 136 (1): 93–99.

Judd, Margaret, and Joel Irish. 2009. "Dying to Serve: The Mass Burials at Kerma." *Antiquity* 83 (321): 709–722.

Carthage and other tophets with infant sacrifice:

Schwartz, J.H., F.D. Houghton, L. Bondioli, and R. Macchiarelli. 2012. "Bones, Teeth, and Estimating Age of Perinates: Carthaginian Infant Sacrifice Revisited." *Antiquity* 86 (333): 738–745.

Smith, P., G. Avishai, J.A. Greene, and L.E. Stager. 2011. "Aging Cremated Infants: The Problem of Sacrifice at the Tophet of Carthage." *Antiquity* 85 (329): 859–874.

Appendix

Smith, Patricia, Lawrence E. Stager, Joseph A. Greene, and Gal Avishai. 2013. "Cemetery or Sacrifice? Infant Burials at the Carthage Tophet." *Antiquity* 87 (338): 1191–1199.

Xella, Paolo, Josephine Quinn, Valentina Melchiorri, and Peter van Dommelen. 2013. "Cemetery or Sacrifice? Infant Burials at the Carthage Tophet." *Antiquity* 87 (338): 1199–1207.

Asia

Mongolia mortuary sacrifice:

Murail, P., E. Crubézy, H. Martin, L. Haye, J. Bruzek, P.h. Giscard, T. Turbat, and D. Erdenebaatar. 2000. "The Man, the Woman and the Hyoid Bone: From Archaeology to the Burial Practices of the Xiongnu People (Egyin Gol Valley, Mongolia)." *Antiquity* 74 (285): 531–536.

Siberia mortuary sacrifice:

Rudenko, Sergei I. 1970. *Frozen Tombs of Siberia: The Pazyryk Burials of Iron Age Horsemen.* London: J.M. Dent & Sons.

Bibliography

Albert, Jean-Pierre, and Béatrix Midant-Reynes, eds. 2005. *Le sacrifice human en Égypte ancienne et ailleurs*. Paris: Soleb.

Aldhouse Green, Miranda. 2001. *Dying for the Gods: Human Sacrifice in Iron Age and Roman Europe*. Stroud: Tempus.

Aletsee, K.W. 1967. "Datierungsversuch der Moorleichenfunde von Dätgen 1959/1960." *Offa* 24: 79–83.

Andersen, Svend Th. 1987. "The Bog Find from Sigersdal." *Journal of Danish Archaeology* 6 (1): 220–22.

Asingh, Pauline. 2007. "The Magical Bog." In *Grauballe Man: An Iron Age Bog Body Revisited*, edited by Pauline Asingh and Niels Lynnerup, 274–90.

Asingh, Pauline, and Niels Lynnerup, eds. 2007. *Grauballe Man: An Iron Age Bog Body Revisited*. Jutland Archaeological Society Publications 49. Højbjerg: Moesgård Museum and Jutland Archaeological Society.

Baadsgaard, Aubrey, Janet Monge, Samantha Cox, and Richard L. Zettler. 2011. "Human Sacrifice and Intentional Corpse Preservation in the Royal Cemetery of Ur." *Antiquity* 85 (327): 27–42.

Baadsgaard, Aubrey, Janet Monge, and Richard L. Zettler. 2012. "Bludgeoned, Burned, and Beautified: Reevaluating Mortuary Practices in the Royal Cemetery of Ur." In *Sacred Killing*, edited by Anne Porter and Glenn M. Schwartz, 125–58.

Bagley, Robert. 1999. "Shang Archaeology." In *The Cambridge History of Ancient China: From the Origins of Civilization to 221 B.C.*, edited by M. Loewe and E. Shaughnessy, 124–231.

Batres, Leopoldo. 1906. *Teotihuacan*. Mexico, D.F.: Fidencio S. Soria.

Beck, Lane A., and April K. Sievert. 2005. "Mortuary Pathways Leading to the Cenote at Chichén Itzá." In *Interacting with the Dead: Perspectives on*

Mortuary Archaeology for the New Millennium, edited by Gordon F.M. Rakita, Jane E. Buikstra, Lane A. Beck, and Sloan R. Williams, 290–304. Gainesville: University Press of Florida.

Becker, C.J. 1952. "Skeletfundet fra Porsmose ved Næstved." *Nationalmuseets Arbejdsmark* 1952: 25–30.

Bennike, P., and Klaus Ebbesen. 1985. "Stenstrupmanden." *Fra Holbæk Amt*, 28–39.

Bennike, Pia, and Klaus Ebbesen. 1986. "The Bog Find from Sigersdal." *Journal of Danish Archaeology* 5 (1): 85–115.

Bennike, Pia, Klaus Ebbesen, and Lise Bender Jørgensen. 1986. "Early Neolithic Skeletons from Bolkilde Bog, Denmark." *Antiquity* 60 (230): 199–209.

Berryman, Carrie Anne. 2007. "Captive Sacrifice and Trophy Taking among the Ancient Maya: An Evaluation of the Bioarchaeological Evidence and Its Sociopolitical Implications." In *The Taking and Displaying of Human Body Parts as Trophies by Amerindians*, edited by Richard J. Chacon and David H. Dye, 377–99.

Bestock, Laurel. 2011. "The First Kings of Egypt: The Abydos Evidence." In *Before the Pyramids: The Origins of Egyptian Civilization*, edited by Emily Teeter, 137–44.

Bolles, John S. 1977. *Las Monjas: A Major Pre-Mexican Architectural Complex at Chichén Itzá*. Norman: University of Oklahoma Press.

Boone, Elizabeth H., ed. 1984. *Ritual Human Sacrifice in Mesoamerica*. Washington DC: Dumbarton Oaks.

Briggs, C.S. 1995. "Did They Fall or Were They Pushed? Some Unresolved Questions about Bog Bodies." In *Bog Bodies: New Discoveries and New Perspectives*, edited by R.C. Turner and R.G. Scaife, 168–82.

Briggs, C.S., and R.C. Turner. 1986. "A Gazetteer of Bog Burials from Britain and Ireland." In *Lindow Man: The Body in the Bog*, edited by I.M. Stead, J.B. Bourke, and Don Brothwell, 181–95.

Brothwell, Don, D. Liversage, and B. Gottlieb. 1990. "Radiographic and Forensic Aspects of the Female Huldremose Body." *Journal of Danish Archaeology* 9: 157–78.

Bulling, A. Gutkind. 1977. "A Late Shang Place of Sacrifice and Its Historical Significance." *Expedition* Summer 1977: 4–11.

Campbell, Roderick. 2014. *Archaeology of the Chinese Bronze Age: From Erlitou to Anyang*. Los Angeles: Cotsen Institute of Archaeology.

Carlson, John B. 2013. "Chacmool: Who Was That Enigmatic Recumbent Figure from Epiclassic Mesoamerica? Reposing the Question." *The Smoking Mirror* 21 (4): 2–7.

Carrasco Vargas, Ramón, Sylvia Boucher, Paula Alvarez González, Vera Tiesler, Valeria García Vierna, Renata García Moreno, and Javier Vázquez Negrete. 1999. "A Dynastic Tomb from Campeche, Mexico: New Evidence on Jaguar Paw, a Ruler of Calakmul." *Latin American Antiquity* 10 (1): 47–58.

Carter, Jeffrey, ed. 2003. *Understanding Religious Sacrifice: A Reader*. London and New York: Continuum.

Chacon, Richard J., and David H. Dye, eds. 2007. *The Taking and Displaying of Human Body Parts as Trophies by Amerindians*. New York: Springer.

Chang, K.C. 1980. *Shang Civilization*. New Haven and London: Yale University Press.

1986a. *Studies of Shang Archaeology: Selected Papers from the International Conference on Shang Civilization*. New Haven: Yale University Press.

1986b. "Yin-Hsü Tomb Number Five and the Question of the P'an Keng/ Hsiao Hsin/Hsiao Yi Period in Yin-Hsü Archaeology." In *Studies of Shang Archaeology: Selected Papers from the International Conference on Shang Civilization*, edited by K.C. Chang, 65–79.

Chinchilla Mazariegos, Oswaldo. 2014. "Flaying, Dismemberment, and Ritual Human Sacrifice on the Pacific Coast of Guatemala." *The PARI Journal* XIV (3, Winter): 1–12.

Coe, Michael D., and Rex Koontz. 2013. *Mexico: From the Olmecs to the Aztecs.* Seventh edition. London: Thames & Hudson.

Coe, William R. 1959. *Piedras Negras Archaeology: Artifacts, Caches, and Burials.* University Museum, University of Pennsylvania.

Crubézy, Éric, and Béatrix Midant-Reynes. 2005. "Les sacrifices humain à l'époque prédynastique: l'apport de la nécropole d'Adaïma." In *Le sacrifice human en Égypte ancienne et ailleurs*, edited by Jean-Pierre Albert and Béatrix Midant-Reynes, 58–81.

Csorba, Mrea. 1996. "The Chinese Northern Frontier: Reassessment of the Bronze Age Burials from Baifu." *Antiquity* 70 (269): 564–587.

Cucina, Andrea, and Vera Tiesler. 2006. "The Companions of Janaab' Pakal and the 'Red Queen' from Palenque, Chiapas: Meaning of Human Companion Sacrifice in Classic Maya Society." In *Janaab' Pakal of Palenque: Reconstructing the Life and Death of a Maya Ruler*, edited by Vera Tiesler and Andrea Cucina, 102–25. University of Arizona Press.

Demarest, Arthur A. 1984. "Overview: Mesoamerican Human Sacrifice in Evolutionary Perspective." In *Ritual Human Sacrifice in Mesoamerica*, edited by Elizabeth H. Boone, 227–47.

Dickson, D. Bruce. 2006. "Public Transcripts Expressed in Theatres of Cruelty: The Royal Graves at Ur in Mesopotamia." *Cambridge Archaeological Journal* 16 (2): 123–144.

Dieck, Alfred. 1965. *Die europäischen Moorleichenfunde (Hominidenmoorfunde).* Neumünster: Karl Wachholtz Verlag.

Diehl, Richard A. 1983. *Tula: The Toltec Capital of Ancient Mexico.* New Aspects of Antiquity. London: Thames & Hudson.

Dijk, Jacobus van. 2007. "Retainer Sacrifice in Egypt and in Nubia." In *The Strange World of Human Sacrifice*, edited by Jan N. Bremmer, 135–55. Leuven: Peeters.

Dougherty, Sean P., and Renée F. Friedman. 2008. "Sacred or Mundane: Scalping and Decapitation at Predynastic Hierakonpolis." In *Egypt at Its Origins 2. Proceedings of the International Conference "Origin of the State. Predynastic and Early Dynastic Egypt,"* edited by Béatrix Midant-Reynes and Y. Tristant, 311–38.

Dreyer, Günter. 1990. "Umm el-Qaab: Nachuntersuchungen im frühzeitlichen Königsfriedhof." *Mitteilungen des Deutschen Archäologischen Instituts, Abteilung Kairo* 46: 53–90.

———. 2011. "Tomb U-J: A Royal Burial of Dynasty 0 at Abydos." In *Before the Pyramids: The Origins of Egyptian Civilization*, edited by Emily Teeter, 127–36.

Duncan, William N. 2011. "Bioarchaeological Analysis of Sacrificial Victims from a Postclassic Maya Temple from Ixlu, El Peten, Guatemala." *Latin American Antiquity* 22 (4): 549–72.

Earwood, Caroline. 1997. "Bog Butter: A Two Thousand Year History." *The Journal of Irish Archaeology* 8: 25–42.

Ediger, Donald. 1971. *The Well of Sacrifice*. Garden City, NY: Doubleday & Company.

Ellis, Ann Grosvenor, and B. Westley. 1964. "Preliminary Report on the Animal Remains in the Jericho Tombs." In *Excavations at Jericho, Vol. II: The Tombs Excavated in 1955–8*, by Kathleen Kenyon, 694–96.

Ellis, Richard S. 1968. *Foundation Deposits in Ancient Mesopotamia*. New Haven: Yale University Press.

Emery, Walter B. 1954. *Excavations at Sakkara: Great Tombs of the First Dynasty II*. London: Egypt Exploration Society.

———. 1961. *Archaic Egypt*. Middlesex: Penguin.

Fagan, Garrett G. 2006. *Archaeological Fantasies: How Pseudoarchaeology Misrepresents the Past and Misleads the Public*. Abingdon: Psychology Press.

Falkenhausen, Lothar von. 1999. "The Waning of the Bronze Age: Material Culture and Social Developments, 770–481 B.C." In *The Cambridge History of Ancient China: From the Origins of Civilization to 221 B.C.*, edited by M. Loewe and E. Shaughnessy, 450–544.

Fischer, Christian. 1980a. "Døden og mosen." *Skalk* 4: 18–26.

   1980b. "Moseligene fra Bjældskovdal." *KUML* 1979: 7–44.

Fitzsimmons, James L. 2009. *Death and the Classic Maya Kings*. Austin: University of Texas Press.

Fowler, William R. 1984. "Late Preclassic Mortuary Patterns and Evidence for Human Sacrifice at Chalchuapa, El Salvador." *American Antiquity* 49 (3): 603–18.

Frazer, James George. 1993. *The Golden Bough: A Study in Magic and Religion*. Ware: Wordsworth.

Frei, Karin Margarita, Ulla Mannering, Kristian Kristiansen, Morten E. Allentoft, Andrew S. Wilson, Irene Skals, Silvana Tridico, Marie Louise Nosch, Eske Willerslev, Leon Clarke and Robert Frei 2015a. "Tracing the Dynamic Life Story of a Bronze Age Female." *Scientific Reports* 5 (10431).

Frei, Karin Margarita, Ulla Mannering, T. Douglas Price, and Rasmus Birch Iversen. 2015b. "Strontium Isotope Investigations of the Haraldskær Woman – a Complex Record of Various Tissues." *ArcheoSciences. Revue D'archéométrie*, no. 39 (December): 93–101.

Friedman, Renée F. 2008a. "Excavating Egypt's Early Kings: Recent Discoveries in the Elite Cemetery at Hierakonpolis." In *Egypt at Its Origins 2. Proceedings of the International Conference "Origin of the State. Predynastic and Early Dynastic Egypt, "* edited by Béatrix Midant-Reynes and Y. Tristant, 1157–94.

   2008b. "The Cemeteries of Hierakonpolis." *Archéo-Nil* 18: 8–29.

   2011. "Hierakonpolis." In *Before the Pyramids: The Origins of Egyptian Civilization*, edited by Emily Teeter, 33–44.

Friedman, Renée F., Wim van Neer, Bea de Cupere, Javier Droux, Anna Pieri, Sean P. Dougherty, and Daniel Antoine. 2017. "The Elite Predynastic Cemtery at Hierakonpolis HK6: 2011–2015 Progress Report. With Appendix: Demographic Survey of HK6." In *Egypt at Its Origins 5*, edited by Béatrix Midant-Reynes and Yann Tristant. Leuven, Paris, Bristol: Peeters.

Galvin, John. 2005. "Abydos: New Evidence Shows That, Human Sacrifice Helped Populate the Royal City of the Dead." *National Geographic Magazine*, April.

Gansell, Amy Rebecca. 2007. "Identity and Adornment in the Third-Millennium BC Mesopotamian 'Royal Cemetery' at Ur." *Cambridge Archaeological Journal* 17 (1): 29–46.

Gebühr, Michael. 1979. "Das Kindergrab von Windeby." *Offa* 36: 75–107.

Gibson, McGuire. 1972. *The City and Area of Kish*. Miami: Field Research Projects.

Girard, René. 1986. *The Scapegoat*. Translated by Yvonne Freccero. Baltimore: Johns Hopkins University Press.

2005. *Violence and the Sacred*. Translated by Patrick Gregory. London: Continuum.

Glob, P.V. 1969. *The Bog People: Iron-Age Man Preserved*. Translated by Rupert Bruce-Mitford. London: Faber and Faber.

Green, Alberto Ravinell Whitney. 1975. *The Role of Human Sacrifice in the Ancient Near East*. Missoula, Montana: Scholars Press.

Gregersen, Markil. 1980. "Moseliget fra Elling: En retsmedicinsk undersøgelse." *KUML* 1979: 45–57.

Gregersen, Markil, Anne Grethe Jurik, and Niels Lynnerup. 2007. "Forensic Evidence, Injuries and Cause of Death." In *Grauballe Man: An Iron Age Bog Body Revisited*, edited by Pauline Asingh and Niels Lynnerup, 234–58.

Grüner, Oskar. 1979. "Die 'Moorleiche' von Windeby." *Offa* 36: 116–18.

Hankey, Vronwy. 1974a. "A Late Bronze Age Temple at Amman: I. The Aegean Pottery." *Levant* 6 (1): 131–59.

1974b. "A Late Bronze Age Temple at Amman: II. Vases and Objects Made of Stone." *Levant* 6 (1): 160–78.

Harrison-Buck, Eleanor, Patricia A. McAnany, and Rebecca Storey. 2007. "Empowered and Disempowered during the Late to Terminal Classic Transition: Maya Burial and Termination Rituals in the Sibun Valley, Belize." In *New Perspectives on Human Sacrifice and Ritual Body Treatments in Ancient Maya Society*, edited by Vera Tiesler and Andrea Cucina, 75–101.

Hayen, Hajo. 1964. "Die Knabenmoorleiche aus dem Kayhausener Moor 1922." *Oldenburger Jahrbuch* 63: 19–42.

Heinemeier, Jan, and Pauline Asingh. 2007. "Dating of Grauballe Man." In *Grauballe Man: An Iron Age Bog Body Revisited*, edited by Pauline Asingh and Niels Lynnerup, 196–201.

Hennessy, J.B. 1966. "Excavation of a Late Bronze Age Temple at Amman." *Palestine Exploration Quarterly* 108: 155–62.

1985. "Thirteenth Century B.C. Temple of Human Sacrifice at Amman." In *Phoenica and Its Neighbours*, edited by Eric Gubel and E. Lipiński, 85–104. Studia Phoenicia, III. Leuven: Peeters.

Herr, Larry G. 1981. "Ancient Crematorium Discovered?" *Ministry* November: 24–25.

1983. "The Amman Airport Structure and the Geopolitics of Ancient Transjordan." *The Biblical Archaeologist* 46 (4): 223–29.

Hikade, Thomas, and Jane Roy. 2015. "Human Sacrifice in Pre- and Early Dynastic Egypt: What Do You Want to Find?" In *Not Sparing the Child: Human Sacrifice in the Ancient World and beyond*, edited by Daphna Arbel, Paul C. Burns, J.R.C. Cousland, Richard Menkis, and Dietmar Neufeld, 18–49. London: Bloomsbury.

Hoffman, Michael A. 1984. *Egypt before the Pharaohs: The Prehistoric Foundations of Egyptian Civilization*. New York: Alfred A. Knopf.

Hubert, Henri, and Marcel Mauss. 1964. *Sacrifice: Its Nature and Functions*. Chicago: University of Chicago Press.

Hvass, Lone. 1998. *Dronning Gunhild – et Moselig fra Jernalderen*. Vejle: Sesam.

Jay, Nancy. 1992. *Throughout Your Generations Forever: Sacrifice, Religion, and Paternity*. London: University of Chicago Press.

Joy, Jody. 2009. *Lindow Man*. London: British Museum Press.

Kaiser, Werner. 1964. "Einige Bemerkungen zur ägyptischen Frühzeit." *Zeitschrift für Ägyptische Sprache* 91 (2): 86–125.

Keightley, David N. 1979. "The Shang State as Seen in the Oracle-Bone Inscriptions." *Early China* 5: 25–34.

1999. "The Shang: China's First Historical Dynasty." In *The Cambridge History of Ancient China: From the Origins of Civilization to 221 B.C.*, edited by M. Loewe and E. Shaughnessy, 232–91.

Kelly, Eamonn P. 2012a. "An Archaeological Interpretation of Irish Iron Age Bog Bodies." In *The Archaeology of Violence: Interdisciplinary Approaches*, edited by Sarah Ralph, 232–40. New York: State University of New York Press.

2012b. "The Bog Body from Cashel Bog, Co. Laois." *Ossory, Laois and Leinster* 5: 1–18.

Kelly-Buccellati, Marilyn. 2002. "Ein hurritischer Gang in die Unterwelt." *Mitteilungen der Deutschen Orient-Gesellschaft zu Berlin* 134: 131–48.

2005. "Introduction to the Archaeo-Zoology of the Abi." *Studi Micenei Ed Egeo-Anatolici* 47: 61–66.

Kenyon, Kathleen M. 1960. *Excavations at Jericho I: The Tombs Excavated in 1952–4*. London: British School of Archaeology in Jerusalem.

1964. *Excavations at Jericho, Vol. II: The Tombs Excavated in 1955–8*. London: British School of Archaeology in Jerusalem.

Langfeldt, Bent, and Jørn Raahede. 1980. "Moseliget fra Elling: Røntgenundersøgelse." *KUML* 1979: 59–66.

Li, Chi. 1977. *Anyang*. Seattle: University of Washington Press.

Loewe, M., and E. Shaughnessy, eds. 1999. *The Cambridge History of Ancient China: From the Origins of Civilization to 221 B.C.* New York: Cambridge University Press.

López Luján, Leonardo, and Judy Levin. 2006. *Tenochtitlan*. Oxford: Oxford University Press.

Ludes, Bertrand, and Éric Crubézy. 2005. "Le sacrifice humain en contexte funéraire: problèmes posés à l'anthropologie et à la médicine légale. L'exemple prédynastique." In *Le sacrifice human en Égypte ancienne et ailleurs*, edited by Jean-Pierre Albert and Béatrix Midant-Reynes, 82–95.

Lund, Allan A. 1976. *Moselig*. Aarhus: Wormianum.

2002. *Mumificerede Moselig*. Copenhagen: Høst & Søn.

Magilton, J.R. 1995. "Lindow Man: The Celtic Tradition and beyond." In *Bog Bodies: New Discoveries and New Perspectives*, edited by R.C. Turner and R.G. Scaife, 183–87.

Maish, A., and R. Friedman. 1999. "Pondering Paddy: Unwrapping the Mysteries of HK43." *Nekhen News* 11: 6–7.

Mallowan, M.E.L. 1947. "Excavations at Brak and Chagar Bazar." *Iraq* 9: 1–259.

Mannering, Ulla, Karin Margarita Frei, Anne Lisbeth Schmidt, and Irene Skals. 2011. "Huldremosekvinden – Nyt Liv i Gamle Klæder." *Nationalmuseets Arbejdsmark* 2011: 33–45.

Marchesi, Gianni. 2004. "Who Was Buried in the Royal Tombs of Ur? Epigraphic and Textual Data." *Orientalia* 73: 153–97.

Marchetti, Nicolò, and Lorenzo Nigro. 1997. "Cultic Activities in the Sacred Area of Ishtar at Ebla during the Old Syrian Period: The 'Favissae' F.5327 and F.5238." *Journal of Cuneiform Studies* 49: 1–44.

Matos Moctezuma, Eduardo. 1988. *The Great Temple of the Aztecs: Treasures of Tenochtitlan*. London: Thames & Hudson.

Matthews, Roger, ed. 2003. *Excavations at Tell Brak. Vol. 4: Exploring an Upper Mesopotamian Regional Centre, 1994–1996*. London: British School of Archaeology in Iraq.

McAnany, Patricia A. 1995. *Living with the Ancestors: Kinship and Kingship in Ancient Maya Society*. Austin: University of Texas Press.

Mendoza, Rubén G. 2007a. "Aztec Militarism and Blood Sacrifice." In *Latin American Indigenous Warfare and Ritual Violence*, edited by Richard J. Chacon and Rubén G. Mendoza, 34–54. Tucson: University of Arizona Press.

2007b. "The Divine Gourd Tree: Tzompantli Skull Racks, Decapitation Rituals, and Human Trophies in Ancient Mesoamerica." In *The Taking and Displaying of Human Body Parts as Trophies by Amerindians*, edited by Richard J. Chacon and David H. Dye, 400–443.

Menu, Bernadette. 2005. "Mise à mort cérémonielle et prélèvements royaux sous la Ire dynastie (Narmer-Den)." In *Le sacrifice human en Égypte ancienne et ailleurs*, edited by Jean-Pierre Albert and Béatrix Midant-Reynes, 122–35.

Midant-Reynes, Béatrix, and Y. Tristant, eds. 2008. *Egypt at Its Origins 2. Proceedings of the International Conference "Origin of the State. Predynastic and Early Dynastic Egypt."* Leuven: Peeters.

Miller, Mary Ellen. 1985. "A Re-Examination of the Mesoamerican Chacmool." *The Art Bulletin* 67 (1): 7–17.

2001. *The Art of Mesoamerica: From Olmec to Aztec*. Third edition. London: Thames & Hudson.

Miller, Virginia E. 1999. "The Skull Rack in Mesoamerica." In *Mesoamerican Architecture as a Cultural Symbol*, edited by Jeff Karl Kowalski, 340–366. New York and Oxford: Oxford University Press.

2007. "Skeletons, Skulls, and Bones in the Art of Chichén Itzá." In *New Perspectives on Human Sacrifice and Ritual Body Treatments in Ancient Maya Society*, edited by Vera Tiesler and Andrea Cucina, 165–89.

Millon, René. 1992. "Teotihuacan Studies: From 1950 to 1990 and beyond." In *Art, Ideology, and the City of Teotihuacan*, edited by Janet Catherine Berlo, 339–419. Washington, D.C.: Dumbarton Oaks.

Molleson, Theya. 2001. "A Note on the Human Skeletal Material from Area FS." In *Excavations at Tell Brak. Vol. 2: Nagar in the Third Millennium BC*, by David Oates, Joan Oates, and Helen MacDonald, 350–52.

Molleson, Theya, and Dawn Hodgson. 2003. "The Human Remains from Woolley's Excavations at Ur." *Iraq* 65: 91–129.

Moorey, P.R.S. 1978. *Kish Excavations, 1923–1933*. Oxford: Clarendon Press.

Morley, Sylvanus G., and George W. Brainerd. 1983. *The Ancient Maya*. Fourth edition. Stanford, California: Stanford University Press.

Morris, Ellen F. 2014. "(Un)Dying Loyalty: Meditations on Retainer Sacrifice in Ancient Egypt and Elsewhere." In *Violence and Civilization: Studies of Social Violence and Prehistory*, edited by Roderick Campbell. Oxford and Oakville: Oxbow Books.

Moser, Christopher L. 1973. *Human Decapitation in Ancient Mesoamerica*. Dumbarton Oaks: Trustees for Harvard University.

Nielsen, Ole. 2014. *Tollundmanden og Ellingkvinden*. Silkeborg: Silkeborg Museum.

Nigro, Lorenzo. 1998. "A Human Sacrifice Associated with a Sheep Slaughter in the Sacred Area of Ishtar at MB I Ebla?" *Journal of Prehistoric Religion* XI–XII: 22–36.

Ó Floinn, R. 1995a. "Recent Research into Irish Bog Bodies." In *Bog Bodies: New Discoveries and New Perspectives*, edited by R.C. Turner and R.G. Scaife, 137–45.

1995b. "Gazetteer of Bog Bodies in the British Isles. 2 Ireland." In *Bog Bodies: New Discoveries and New Perspectives*, edited by R.C. Turner and R.G. Scaife, 221–34.

Oates, David, Joan Oates, and Helen McDonald. 2001. *Excavations at Tell Brak. Vol. 2: Nagar in the Third Millennium BC*. London: British School of Archaeology in Iraq.

O'Connor, David. 2009. *Abydos: Egypt's First Pharaohs and the Cult of Osiris*. London: Thames & Hudson.

2011. "The Narmer Palette: A New Interpretation." In *Before the Pyramids: The Origins of Egyptian Civilization*, edited by Emily Teeter, 145–52.

Pereira, Grégory, and Ximena Chávez. 2006. "Restos humanos en el Entierro 6 de la Pirámide de la Luna." In *Sacrificios de consagración en La Pirámide de la Luna*, edited by Saburo Sugiyama and Leonardo López Luján, 53–60.

Petrie, W.M. Flinders. 1900. *The Royal Tombs of the First Dynasty: Part I*. London: Egypt Exploration Fund.

1901. *The Royal Tombs of the Earliest Dynasties: Part II*. London: Egypt Exploration Fund.

1907. *Gizeh and Rifeh*. London: School of Archaeology in Egypt.

1914. *Tarkhan II*. London: School of Archaeology in Egypt.

1925. *Tombs of the Courtiers and Oxyrhynkhos*. London: British School of Archaeology in Egypt.

Philipsen, Bent. 1980. "Moseliget fra Elling: En Undersøgelse af Kæbeknogledele og Tandforhold." *KUML* 1979: 67–72.

Piehl, Jennifer C., and Jaime J. Awe. 2010. "Scalping as a Component of Terminus Structure Ritual at the Site of Baking Pot, Belize Valley." *Research Reports in Belizean Archaeology* 7: 55–63.

Pijoan Aguadé, Carmen María, and Josefina Mansilla Lory. 1997. "Evidence for Human Sacrifice, Bone Modification and Cannibalism in Ancient Mexico." In *Troubled Times: Violence and Warfare in the*

Past, edited by Debra L. Martin and David W. Frayer, 217–39. Amsterdam: OPA.

Pollock, Susan, and Reinhard Bernbeck, eds. 2005. *Archaeologies of the Middle East: Critical Perspectives*. Oxford: Blackwell.

Porter, Anne. 2012. "Mortal Mirrors: Creating Kin through Human Sacrifice in Third Millennium Syro-Mesopotamia." In *Sacred Killing*, edited by Anne Porter and Glenn M. Schwartz, 191–215.

Porter, Anne, and Glenn M. Schwartz, eds. 2012. *Sacred Killing: The Archaeology of Sacrifice in the Ancient Near East*. Winona Lake: Eisenbrauns.

Randsborg, Klavs. 1995. *Hjortspring: Warfare and Sacrifice in Early Europe*. Aarhus: Aarhus University Press.

Reade, Julian. 2001. "Assyrian King-Lists, the Royal Tombs of Ur, and Indus Origins." *Journal of Near Eastern Studies* 60 (1): 1–29.

Recht, Laerke. 2014. "Symbolic Order: Liminality and Simulation in Human Sacrifice in the Bronze-Age Aegean and Near East." *Journal of Religion and Violence* 2 (3): 403–32.

Reisner, George Andrew. 1936. *The Development of the Egyptian Tomb down to the Accession of Cheops*. Cambridge: Harvard University Press.

Robicsek, Francis, and Donald M. Hales. 1984. "Maya Heart Sacrifice: Cultural Perspectives and Surgical Technique." In *Ritual Human Sacrifice in Mesoamerica*, edited by Elizabeth H. Boone, 49–90.

Ross, Anne. 1986. "Lindow Man and the Celtic Tradition." In *Lindow Man: The Body in the Bog*, edited by I.M. Stead, J.B. Bourke, and Don Brothwell, 162–69.

Ruppert, Karl. 1952. *Chichen Itza: Architectural Notes and Plans*. Washington, D.C.: Carnegie Institution of Washington.

Sanden, Wijnand van der. 1995. "Bog Bodies on the Continent: Developments since 1965, with Special Reference to the Netherlands." In *Bog Bodies:*

New Discoveries and New Perspectives, edited by R.C. Turner and R.G. Scaife, 146–65.

1996. *Through Nature to Eternity: The Bog Bodies of Northwest Europe.* Amsterdam: Batavian Lion International.

Scarborough, Vernon L., and David R. Wilcox, eds. 1993. *The Mesoamerican Ballgame.* Tucson: University of Arizona Press.

Schele, Linda, and Mary Ellen Miller. 1992. *The Blood of Kings: Dynasty and Ritual in Maya Art.* London: Thames & Hudson.

Schwartz, Glenn M. 2012. "Archaeology and Sacrifice." In *Sacred Killing*, edited by Anne Porter and Glenn M. Schwartz, 1–32.

2013. "Memory and Its Demolition: Ancestors, Animals and Sacrifice at Umm El-Marra, Syria." *Cambridge Archaeological Journal* 23 (3): 495–522.

Schwartz, Glenn M., Hans H. Curvers, Sally Dunham, and Barbara Stuart. 2003. "A Third-Millennium B.C. Elite Tomb and Other New Evidence from Tell Umm El-Marra, Syria." *American Journal of Archaeology* 107 (3): 325–61.

Schwartz, Glenn M., Hans H. Curvers, Sally Dunham, Barbara Stuart, and Jill Ann Weber. 2006. "A Third-Millennium B.C. Elite Mortuary Complex at Umm El-Marra, Syria: 2002 and 2004 Excavations." *American Journal of Archaeology* 110 (4): 603–41.

Sharer, Robert James, and David W. Sedat. 1987. *Archaeological Investigations of the Northern Maya Highlands, Guatemala: Interaction and Development of Maya Civilization.* Philadelphia: University of Pennsylvania Press.

Shelach, Gideon. 1996. "The Qiang and the Question of Human Sacrifice in the Late Shang Period." *Asian Perspectives* 35 (1): 1–26.

Simonsen, Povl. 1953. "To Djurslandske Mosefund fra Keltisk Jernalder." *KUML* 1953: 61–71.

Smith, William Robertson. 2002. *Religion of the Semites*. New Brunswick and London: Transaction Publishers.

Speiser, E.A. 1935. *Excavations at Tepe Gawra. Vol. I: Levels I-VIII*. Philadelphia: University of Pennsylvania Press.

Spence, Michael W., and Grégory Pereira. 2007. "The Human Skeletal Remains of the Moon Pyramid, Teotihuacan." *Ancient Mesoamerica* 18: 147–57.

Starr, Richard Francis Strong. 1939. *Nuzi: Report on the Excavations at Gorgan Tepa near Kirkuk, Iraq. Vol. I*. Cambridge (Mass.): Harvard University Press.

Stead, I.M., J.B. Bourke, and Don Brothwell, eds. 1986. *Lindow Man: The Body in the Bog*. London: British Museum Publications.

Struve, K.W. 1967. "Die Moorleiche von Dätgen: ein Diskussionsbeitrage zur Strafopferthese." *Offa* 24: 33–76.

Sugiyama, Saburo. 2005. *Human Sacrifice, Militarism, and Rulership: Materialization of State Ideology at the Feathered Serpent Pyramid, Teotihuacan*. Cambridge: Cambridge University Press.

Sugiyama, Saburo, and Rubén Cabrera Castro. 2006. "El proyecto pirámide de la Luna 1998–2004: Conclusiones preliminares." In *Sacrificios de consagración en La Pirámide de la Luna*, edited by Saburo Sugiyama and Leonardo López Luján, 11–24.

Sugiyama, Saburo, and Leonardo López Luján, eds. 2006a. *Sacrificios de consagración en La Pirámide de la Luna*. Mexico: Arizona State University.

—— 2006b. "Sacrificios de consagración en La Pirámide de la Luna, Teotihuacan." In *Sacrificios de consagración en La Pirámide de la Luna*, edited by Saburo Sugiyama and Leonardo López Luján, 25–52.

Tang, Jigen. 2004. "*The Social Organization of Late Shang China: A Mortuary Perspective*." PhD, London: University of London.

Tauber, Henrik. 1980. "Kulstof-14 Datering af Moselig." *KUML* 1979: 73–78.

Teeter, Emily, ed. 2011. *Before the Pyramids: The Origins of Egyptian Civilization*. Oriental Institute Publication 33. Chicago: Oriental Institute of the University of Chicago.

Tefnin, R. 1979. "Une ville fortifiée à l'âge du Bronze en Syrie du Nord: Tell Abou Danné." *Archéologia* 129: 42–49.

Thorvilsen, Elise. 1953. "Menneskeofringer i Oldstiden. Jernalderligene fra Borremose i Himmerland." *KUML* 1952: 32–48.

Tiesler, Vera. 2007. "Funerary and Nonfunerary? New References in Identifying Ancient Maya Sacrificial and Postsacrificial Behaviors from Human Assemblages." In *New Perspectives on Human Sacrifice and Ritual Body Treatments in Ancient Maya Society*, edited by Vera Tiesler and Andrea Cucina, 14–44.

Tiesler, Vera, and Andrea Cucina. 2006. "Procedures in Human Heart Extraction and Ritual Meaning: A Taphonomic Assessment of Anthropogenic Marks in Classic Maya Skeletons." *Latin American Antiquity* 17 (4): 493–510.

2007. *New Perspectives on Human Sacrifice and Ritual Body Treatments in Ancient Maya Society*. New York: Springer.

Tobler, Arthur John. 1950. *Excavations at Tepe Gawra. Vol II: Levels IX-XX*. Philadelphia: University of Pennsylvania Press.

Tristant, Yann. 2008. "Deux grands tombeaux du cimetière M d'Abou Rawach (Ire dynastie)." *Archéo-Nil* 18: 131–47.

Tsuneki, Akira, Jamal Hydar, Yutaka Miyake, Sadayuki Akahane, Makoto Arimura, Shin-ichi Nishiyama, Haifa Sha'baan, Tomoko Anezaki, and Sachiko Yano. 1998. "Second Preliminary Report of the Excavations at Tell El-Kerkh (1998), Northwestern Syria." *Bulletin of the Oriental Museum* XIX: 1–28.

Turner, R.C. 1986. "Boggarts, Bogles and Sir Gawain and the Green Knight: Lindow Man and the Oral Tradition." In *Lindow Man: The Body in the Bog*, edited by I.M. Stead, J.B. Bourke, and Don Brothwell, 170–76.

1995. "Gazetteer of Bog Bodies in the British Isles. 1 Britain." In *Bog Bodies: New Discoveries and New Perspectives*, edited by R.C. Turner and R.G. Scaife, 205–20.

Turner, R.C., and R.G. Scaife, eds. 1995. *Bog Bodies: New Discoveries and New Perspectives*. London: British Museum Press.

Tylor, Edward Burnett. 1871. *Primitive Culture: Researches into the Development of Mythology, Philosophy, Religion, Art, and Custom*. London: John Murray.

Vidale, Massimo. 2011. "PG 1237, Royal Cemetery of Ur: Patterns in Death." *Cambridge Archaeological Journal* 21 (3): 427–51.

Vogel, Helga. 2014. "Der Königsfriedhof von Ur und das Problem der so genannten Gefolgschaftsbestattungen." In *Gewalt und Gesellschaft: Dimensionen der Gewalt in ur- und frühgeschichtlicher Zeit*, edited by Thomas Link and Heidi Peter-Röcher, 169–85. Bonn: Rudolf Habelt.

Weber, Jill Ann. 2008. "Elite Equids: Redefining Equid Burials of the Mid- to Late 3rd Millennium BC from Umm El-Marra, Syria." In *Archaeozoology of the Near East*, edited by Emmanuelle Vila, Lionel Gourichon, Alice M. Choyke, and Hijlke Buitenhuis, 499–519. Lyon: Maison de l'Orient et de la Méditerrannée.

Weiss-Krejci, Estella. 2003. "Victims of Human Sacrifice in Multiple Tombs of the Ancient Maya. A Critical Review." In *Antropología de La Eternidad. La Muerte En La Cultura Maya*, edited by Andrés Ciudad Ruiz, Mario Humberto Ruz Sosa, and María Josefa Iglesias Ponce de León, 355–81. Madrid: Sociedad Española de Estudios Mayas, Centro de Estudios Mayas.

Welsh, W.B.M. 1988. *An Analysis of Classic Lowland Maya Burials*. BAR International Series 409. Oxford: BAR.

Wengrow, David. 2007. "Enchantment and Sacrifice in Early Egypt." In *Art's Agency and Art History*, edited by Robin Osborne and Jeremy Tanner, 28–41. Oxford: Blackwell.

Wilkerson, S. Jeffrey K. 1984. "In Search of the Mountain of Foam: Human Sacrifice in Eastern Mesoamerica." In *Ritual Human Sacrifice in Mesoamerica*, edited by Elizabeth H. Boone, 101–32.

Woolley, Leonard. 1934. *Ur Excavations II: The Royal Cemetery*. Philadelphia: University of Pennsylvania Press.

1954. *Excavations at Ur: A Record of Twelve Years' Work*. London: Ernest Benn Limited.

1982. *Ur "of the Chaldees."* London: Herbert Press.

Wright, G.R.H. 1966. "The Bronze Age Temple at Amman." *Zeitschrift Für Die Alttestamentliche Wissenschaft* 78 (3) 351–357.

Wright, Lori E. 2005. "In Search of Yax Nuun Ayiin I: Revisiting the Tikal Project's Burial 10." *Ancient Mesoamerica* 16 (1): 89–100.

Yang, Hsi-chang. 1986. "The Shang Dynasty Cemetery System." In *Studies of Shang Archaeology: Selected Papers from the International Conference on Shang Civilization*, edited by K.C. Chang, 49–63.

Acknowledgements

I am very grateful to the series editors, James Lewis and Margo Kitts, for inviting me to contribute the current volume and encourage me to wander into relatively unknown territory. My greatest thanks go to Emma Saunders, who not only shares my enthusiasm for most things Mesoamerican, but is also a great friend and travel companion. Emma, Caitlin Chaves Yates, Jette Junge, Margo Kitts and an anonymous reviewer have kindly proofread and commented on earlier drafts of this work. Thanks are also due to Wilhelm Jansson and Azael Varas for discussions on and references for the Egyptian material. Finally, a number of people have generously given permission to use illustrations from their studies: these are listed with the relevant images.

Cambridge Elements

Religion and Violence

James R. Lewis
University of Tromsø

James R. Lewis is Professor of Religious Studies at the University of Tromsø, Norway and the author and editor of a number of volumes, including *The Cambridge Companion to Religion and Terrorism*.

Margo Kitts
Hawai'i Pacific University

Margo Kitts edits the *Journal of Religion and Violence* and is Professor and Coordinator of Religious Studies and East-West Classical Studies at Hawai'i Pacific University in Honolulu.

ABOUT THE SERIES

Violence motivated by religious beliefs has become all too common in the years since the 9/11 attacks. Not surprisingly, interest in the topic of religion and violence has grown substantially since then. This Elements series on Religion and Violence addresses this new, frontier topic in a series of ca. fifty individual Elements. Collectively, the volumes will examine a range of topics, including violence in major world religious traditions, theories of religion and violence, holy war, witch hunting, and human sacrifice, among others.

Cambridge Elements

Religion and Violence

Printed in the United States
By Bookmasters